RISKY RELATIONSHIPS

An Insightful Look into Success and Failure in Relationships

By

Dane T. Cunningham

Published by: Embrace Relationships Seminars Inc.
P.O. Box 370124
Decatur, GA 30037

Published by Embrace Relationships Seminars, Inc.
P.O. Box 370124
Decatur, Georgia 30037
Web site: www.embrace-relationships.com
To order additional copies, call 1-866-381-BOOK (2665)

www.xulonpress.com

Table of Contents

Dedication

—⚜—

To my spiritual father, Bishop Eddie L. Long. I have considered how an eagle would feel if he lost his wings. God has given the eagle the gift of wings not only to fly but also to fulfil his purpose. The eagle's very existence depends on his ability to fly through the air not just to seek his food but also to mate.

My spiritual gifts have been like my wings that have helped me to fulfil my purpose in ministry. Like the eagle without wings I fear that I would die without fulfilling my purpose.

I will forever give God praise, honor, and glory for my wings, but you by your example, have inspired me to fly!

Love, your son Dane

Reviews

"By examining the life of King David, *Risky Relationships* delivers paramount wisdom for everyone. To understand the purpose for each of your relationships - whether personal, professional, ministerial, or with a family member we must ensure that God is always first. *Risky Relationships* will show you how to do just that."

Bishop Eddie L. Long, Senior Pastor
New Birth Missionary Baptist Church, Lithonia, Georgia

"It's all about relationships! Each one holding this book is a product of some type of a relationship - you didn't get here by your self. The same is true of where you are in life today - someone (relationships) brought you here. *Risky Relationships* not only unpacks the types of relationships, but lifts relationships to a higher and functional level. You will see yourself and others described in these pages, but it won't leave you where you are. Read this book and transform your life."

Dr. Samuel R. Chand, Chancellor
Beulah Heights Bible College, Atlanta, Georgia

"Dane Cunningham has been anointed to speak to the nation regarding relationships. In *Risky Relationships*, Dane takes a comprehensive look at the things we should and should not do in order to have relationships that are healthy and fulfilling. Whether single or married, in ministry, or in corporate America, this book is a great tool in avoiding risky relationships."

Pastor Jerry F. Hutchins
Timothy Baptist Church, Athens, Georgia

"Elder Dane Cunningham has captured the true essence of the biblical principles of relationships. His book outlines the reasons for relationship failures, and provides a spiritual blueprint on relationship success. This book is a must read for all persons currently in relationships who are trying to understand how to deal, handle, and adjust to the various relationships in their daily lives while maintaining and applying God's biblical principles."

Pastor Jesse Curney III
New Mercies Christian Church, Lilburn, Georgia

Introduction

⬥⬥⬥

Have you ever made a bad choice in your relationships? Unless you live on the moon I am sure that the answer is yes. The reason we did not make the best choices in those relationships is because we took unnecessary risks. If a builder constructs an office tower without a foundation the office tower will have an insufficient ability to stand. If the office tower should fall there would likely be injuries and a loss of life as well as a great deal of property damage. Likewise when we are building relationships we can avoid unnecessary risk if we build on the correct foundation.

In 1941, the United States government allied itself with the Soviet dictator Joseph Stalin over the German dictator Adolf Hitler. That alliance was part of the reason for the ending of WWII in Europe. After the end of the war Joseph Stalin turned on the United States because he wanted all of Eastern Europe to be communist, this began the era we now know as the Cold War.

In 1983 the United States government allied itself with Panamanian strong man Manuel Noriega over the Cuban dictator Fidel Castro. Manuel Noriega betrayed the United States by trafficking in illegal drugs and selling military secrets to Communist countries.

In 1980 the United States government allied itself with Sadamm Hussein the president of Iraq over the Ayatollah Khomeni who was the leader of Iran. Later, Sadamm Hussein would lose the Gulf War and violate United Nations sanctions against him, which led to war.

God has created everything through His son, Jesus Christ; therefore He is our foundation. The United States allied with people based on political reasons that excluded God as their foundation therefore those relationship choices were a risk. If given the choice between Joseph Stalin and Adolf Hitler, or Manuel Noriega and Fidel Castro, or Sadamm Hussein and Ayatollah Khomeni we would choose whom we believed was the lesser of the two evils, but what would the foundation be for the choices that we made? History has shown us that our past relationship choices will inevitably impact our future. The foreign policy of the United States government has taught us that a friend today can be an enemy tomorrow. Perhaps our relationship choices are not as dramatic but just like the United States government most of us make relationship choices based on our own selfish agenda which not only puts ourselves but others at unnecessary risk.

In Risky Relationships we will examine the biblical character of David. When David was focused on God as his foundation along with his purpose his relationship choices were a blessing, but when David was distracted by his selfish desires his relationship choices hurt him and others.

When I began to study David's life, I found many similarities between his life and my own. I have had both success and failure in my relationships. In retrospect all my successful relationships were rooted in my pursuit of God and His purpose for my life. Conversely, all my failures in relationships were contrary to God and His purpose for my life. Has not your life been the same?

How many of us can honestly say we understand relationships from the biblical perspective? Many of us probably do not. This is an important point because history has shown us that apart from God all of our relationship choices will be inferior. This is because we cannot bring to a relationship something that we are not. Therefore some of the relationship challenges that we have are really unresolved issues that we project onto the people we are in relationships with. Did you realize that your horizontal relationships with others are a reflection of your vertical relationship with God? God uses our relationships with others to expose where we are with Him. If the truth were told most of our relationship mistakes are based on ignorance about what God says about relationships. The purpose of this book is to show us how we can avoid "Risky Relationships" and have successful relationships in Christ using biblical principles. Whether you are married or single, whether your relationship challenges fall into the family or professional category I believe that there is truth contained in this book that will give you a better understanding about all types of adult relationships.

Join me as we look at David's life and allow the Holy Spirit to minister to you that there is hope for our relationships.

CHAPTER ONE

Relationship Priorities

(The Vertical Relationship First)

Have you ever wondered if you were like a piranha? The answer will surprise you. The piranha is a freshwater fish that lives in the lakes, rivers, and streams of South America. They fulfill their purpose of balancing their environment by feeding on aquatic animals and other fish. They are effective because they travel in groups called schools; this enables them to take down prey much larger than themselves. If you remove the piranha from the water, it will eventually die because the water is its primary source. The piranha uses its razor sharp teeth to accomplish its purpose of eating weaker fish and marine animals. The piranha is a cannibal that will eat other piranha when there is no other food available. The water unites the piranha that swim in schools together, which is their common source of life. The satisfaction of the piranha's hunger is their common sense of purpose.

Our vertical relationship with God is primary because He is our source and apart from Him we can only have temporal success. It is through our relationship with God that He reveals to us our divine purpose. It is through our connection with God that we not only understand our purpose but we are led to develop horizontal relationships that not only glorify God but they help facilitate our purpose.

Like the piranha, we risk dying apart from God who is our source. Life not only has meaning staying vertically connected to our source but also in fulfilling our purpose. If we do not fulfill our purpose we risk a form of spiritual death. We risk failing at our purpose unless we have God-ordained horizontal relationships that help facilitate that purpose. Apart from our purpose we have the potential to hurt those we are in relationships with when we don't have a common sense of purpose that binds us together. In this chapter, we will look at our relationship priorities: which are our vertical connection to God, our purpose, and horizontal relationships that are connected to that purpose.

Our Connection to God

When we are joined to God through faith in Jesus Christ we are connected to Him. In 1 Samuel 13:14, we are told that God was searching for "a man after His own heart." Historically, God ruled His people through men called Judges. Eventually the people grew to a place where they wanted to be ruled by a king like other nations. Samuel was leading the people at the time and he warned them of the consequences of their request but they insisted. In response, God told Samuel to anoint Saul as king. Saul was an attractive man but he did not have a heart after God. Therefore, he was disobedient to God and subsequently forfeited the privilege to rule the people of God. Later David would be anointed king and rule God's people not because he would never be disobedient but because in his heart he desired an intimate relationship with God. In Psalm 95:3-5, we are told:

For the Lord is the great God, and the great King above all Gods. In His hand are the deep places of the earth; the heights of the hills are His also. The sea is His, for He made it; and His hands formed the dry land.

God should have a relationship with all of us because He is our Creator but He only becomes our Father after we accept Jesus Christ as Lord and Savior. Atheists not only reject Jesus as the Son of God but they also reject God as their Creator. All we have to do is look at the sun that shines or watch the beauty of the seasons changing to know that there is a power greater than us that is responsible for all that we behold.

Over 25 years ago after serving in the United States Air Force for four years, I found myself as a 22-year-old young man with plenty of time on my hands. I was fortunate enough to get a good job as an Ohio State Trooper, which enabled me to afford a nice apartment and a decent car. In my spare time, I found myself going from nightclub to nightclub and woman to woman. In chasing women, from time to time I even caught a few. I must admit I had a good time and had enough fun for ten people. Yet there was something missing. After a brief period of listening to an evangelist on Christian television, I accepted Jesus Christ as my Lord and Savior. I later realized that no matter how much I enjoyed my playboy lifestyle, what I really needed was a relationship with God. Although God was my creator apart from my acceptance of His son, Jesus, He was not my Father. I came to understand that I could only have the intimacy that I desired with God through His Son Jesus Christ.

Salvation

During the Old Testament dispensation, a relationship with God was primarily based on the covenant of Abraham.

God promised He would be with the descendants of Abraham, which later became known as the Israelites. Judaism subsequently became the religion of the Israelites. Those who were not Israelites could convert to Judaism by acknowledging the one and only true God of Abraham. They would also have to repent of their past idolatry and keep the laws and traditions of the Israelites.

We now live in the New Testament dispensation where our relationship with God is not based on being a descendant of Abraham or keeping religious traditions but on faith in Jesus Christ , the Son of God. God gave His son, Jesus, as the ultimate sacrifice for man's sin. Under the Old Testament system of worship, sin was atoned for by the sacrifice of animals but when Jesus died on the cross at Calvary and rose from the dead on the third day, He opened the door for all people to come to Him in faith. In Romans 10:9-10, it says:

> *That if you confess with your mouth the Lord Jesus and believe in your heart that God has raised Him from the dead, you will be saved. For with the heart one believes unto righteousness and with the mouth confession is made unto salvation.*

Are you stressed at work? Did your marriage end in divorce? Perhaps all is not well between you and your children or there is some deficiency in your relationships because you have neglected God, who is your source. All things have the same fundamental nature of their source, which is the reason they need to stay connected to that source. Plants need to stay connected to the dirt that is their source. Fish need to stay connected to water, which is its source, and man needs to stay connected to God who is his source. The only way to stay connected to that source is through Jesus Christ. Failure to accept the salvation that God offers through Jesus Christ is to live an eternity apart from God.

Regardless as to whether you are saved or not, you can be disconnected from your source through the distractions of life. When we allow our focus to be horizontal on our issues and not vertical on God, it is inevitable that we will stumble. If one of the parties in a marriage, due to the distractions of life, neglects the sexual intimacy needs of their partner, are they still married? The answer is yes because their relationship is based on their covenant agreement to love one another not their level of sexual intimacy. In the same way, we must understand that our relationship with God is based on our faith in Jesus Christ not how intimate we are with Him at any given point in our journey. Our relationship and intimacy with God is undergirded when we do the following:

Worship
We worship God by sacrificing our will to His will. Our worship is more than a slow song on Sunday morning in church. It is a heartfelt attitude that compels the believer to bow in the presence of the Almighty God.

Praise
We praise God by taking our focus off of ourselves and celebrating His greatness. We praise Him by singing songs that point to Him, lifting our hands to Him, and dancing before Him.

Prayer
We pray to God when we talk to Him about the needs of others and our own concerns. We seek Him for guidance in our lives and in the lives of others.

Studying the Word

We study God's word when we prayerfully approach the Bible to get a better understanding about God and how He desires us to conduct the affairs of our life. There is a difference between studying and reading. When we read, we simply perceive what is being said on paper. When we study, we research what we have read to gain a better understanding.

Meditation

We meditate on God when we silently focus on the reason we worship. We focus on why we praise God. We reflect upon what we have prayed for and we give great thought to what God is saying to us through His word.

Spiritual Idolatry

If you came home and saw your spouse in bed with the mailman, what would you do? If you had enough love to forgive them, what would you do if after a period of healing you caught your spouse in bed with the same mailman again? God is like our husband and we are His spouse, every time we put something ahead of Him it is like committing an act of adultery. The mailman delivers the mail but he does not provide for the household or take care of the children. In the same way, God does for us more than the mailman because He is our all in all. *Spiritual Idolatry* is more than bowing down to a graven image as recorded in the Old Testament it is putting any person, place, or thing ahead of God and His purpose for your life. We can avoid spiritual idolatry when we regularly worship, praise, study, and meditate on God's word.

Have you ever been more concerned about what you do than who gave you the ability to do it? Many of us give more dedication to our work than we do to our God. It is common for ambition to take over but to put your work ahead of God is a form of idolatry. Most ministers are known for doing the work of The Lord, yet excluding Him as the Lord of the work.

If you don't sense the presence of God in your life, do you weep? If you were to lose your child, spouse, or a best friend you would probably have a fit and God would get put on the back burner of your heart. This is spiritual idolatry. It is understood that life is full of challenges, we have to work to survive and we have responsibility to the people we have relationships with, but we should set aside daily time to focus on God. This devotional time could be the first thing in the morning or on the way to work we can listen to Christian music or just meditate on Him. Some of us will need to set aside time at the end of our day but whenever or however you feel led, we need to make time for God, who makes all things possible.

No matter what type of relationship we are concerned about, we must keep God first because He alone is our source.

The Holy Spirit

Have you ever felt that a relationship was wrong for you? That uncomfortable gut feeling may have been the conviction of the Holy Spirit. The Holy Spirit is the invisible person of God who abides within the human spirit of the believer. He is essential to our relationship with God because He leads us to worship, praise, prayer, studying the word, and meditation by giving us a hunger deep within that can only be satisfied by seeking Him. It is very likely that the conviction you experienced in your last bad relationship was because the Holy Spirit knew that you would make that relationship an idol and He was giving you a warning. Sometimes we put our desires ahead of God's purpose for our lives and we need to be redirected on the proper course.

The Holy Spirit is essential in guiding us in our relationship choices. He knows who and what is best for us; therefore, He provides guidance for us to help us make decisions. That guidance may come in the form of doors to certain relationship opportunities being closed and other opportunities being open. If we maintain a prayerful open heart, our divine direction will be clear.

On occasion we will experience a heavy burden from within compelling us to form relationships. Sometimes this burden may feel like a magnet is drawing you to that person. If you have had this experience it could be the Holy Spirit leading you to build a relationship with that person. Be careful because that same burden to establish a relationship may be motivated by your loneliness to establish a personal relationship or your ambition in establishing a professional relationship. We can discern the difference between God's motivation and our motivation simply by asking God to expose to us the hidden thoughts and intents of our heart.

Sometimes we are out of fellowship with God due to the idolatry of keeping sin in our lives or simply pursuing our own agenda. If we insist on going our own way, then we will reap the consequences of our disobedience but the Holy Spirit will always warn us. This is why it is imperative that we keep God first so that we will avoid the unintended consequences of disobedience.

Our Connection to Our Purpose

When we are joined to the realization of why we have been created we are connected to our purpose. In 1 Samuel 16:13, we see that David is anointed king. This presents a couple of challenges for David. First, Saul is still king. Second, David is still a teenager and is too young to take the responsibility of the throne of Israel. David was being prepared by God to do what he had been purposed for. David's life illustrates that our purpose flows from our source, which is God. God prepares us to do what He has created us for long before it comes to pass. David's secular purpose was that of a shepherd and later he became a captain in Saul's army. Conversely, David's spiritual purpose was to be a musician and King of Israel. Both David's secular and spiritual purposes were inextricably connected. They also took an extended period of time before they would be fully realized. In Ecclesiastes 3:1 we are told:

> *To every thing there is a season, a time to*
> *every purpose under the heaven.*

Purpose is the reason why God created you. God did not create us just to exist but to
do something specific that would ultimately lead back to Him. In order for you to fully operate in your purpose, there needs to be a season where God prepares you to do what He has called you to do.

David is one of my favorite Bible characters because I can identify with his strengths and weaknesses. Although I have never had anyone killed like David had Uriah killed, I have allowed my lust for women to hinder my relationship with God like David did with Bathsheba. I can also identify with his secular and spiritual purpose. My secular purpose manifested in my becoming a law enforcement supervisor. My spiritual purpose manifested in my becoming a minister and author. It took twelve years to receive my secular promotion and fourteen years to write and publish my first book. I asked God why it took so long considering I recognized Him as my source. He revealed to me that there was a difference between my season of preparation and my season of operation and that I was not ready to walk in the fullness of what He had purposed for me.

The Season of Preparation

Are you sometimes frustrated at work? Do you wonder why it is taking so long for God to do what He said He was going to do? More than likely it is because you are in a season of preparation.

God is omnipresent which means He is everywhere at the same time all the time. Since God is invisible, He created the visible boundaries we know as night and day. Between every sunrise and sunset is a period of time we call a day. Within each day, God has a specific purpose, which He can be seen in with the spiritual eye as long as we keep the vertical focus of Him being our source. In each day, there is something God desires us to do to prepare for our season of operation.

Perhaps you need to go to the library to research that particular area of interest that has been in the back of your mind for quite some time. If you do not have a computer at home, most public libraries have computers with Internet access that can give you a start to finding the materials that you will need to assist you in discovering your purpose. Perhaps you are already walking in your purpose but you have not developed your skill enough to do it professionally. This may require you seek academic training or maybe even volunteering your time in order to perfect your craft.

In your season of preparation, it is important to understand you may be eligible but not qualified. A fourteen-year-old girl after puberty is eligible to become a mother but is she qualified? A thirty-year-old man without a job is eligible to be a husband but is he qualified? The answer to both questions is no. Once you discover what God has purposed you to do in your secular or spiritual vocation, you are eligible but the question remains are you qualified? If you have not realized the fullness of your purpose, it is probably because you are not qualified. Therefore you should submit to the leading of the Holy Spirit who will direct you to the people, places, and things that will help prepare you for your purpose. I would rather be prepared for my purpose than have my purpose without the necessary preparation.

The Season of Solitude

Have you ever been in a room of people and felt all alone? At times, the company that we find comfort in whether it is our spouse, our family, or our friends is not enough. If you are experiencing this, it may be due to God pruning you so that you may walk in the fullness of your purpose. Our relationships are like a double-edged sword; they can cut for us or cut against us. Your spouse, family, and friends may be a necessary component in the facilitation of your purpose but they can also be a distraction to discerning God's voice.

If you are married, do not be alarmed at moments of solitude in your relationship. If you are a parent do not be surprised if your children withdraw from you at some point. If you are single do not rush out and seek companionship without first seeking God about your season of solitude. There are things God wants to work in you and out of you by yourself. There are things He wants to put in you and take out of you within your relationships. Those things will be revealed to you when you seek after Him with your whole heart.

Well, you ask, how long is the season of solitude? There is no equation or formula to indicate how long this may last. God's purpose is to simply draw you closer to Him. How long is determined by your level of maturity and what God is preparing you for. In the same way that the flowers begin to die in the fall yet they bloom again in spring, so too shall your season of solitude be within your relationships. Be encouraged because this time is an intimate time for you and God that will prepare you for your purpose.

The Season of Operation

In the same way that high school precedes college and the minor leagues precede the major leagues, we have to learn how to crawl before we walk. The time that God has given you to find His purpose or to grow you into that purpose is the time we should take advantage of the opportunities that are available. Those opportunities are sometimes manifested through the challenges of life. So often we perceive the adversity of an illness or job layoff as negative when God may have allowed the experience to be used as a frame of reference during your season of operation. When we understand God as our source, we see that He has a plan that transcends our way of thinking. Has it been difficult for you to get a job? Unemployment is not necessarily a sign of something wrong with you. Sometimes God will deliberately frustrate your attempts to find work because you are attempting to do the wrong thing. Sometimes God will frustrate your attempts to find work because He wants you to know that He is your provider and bring you into another level of intimacy in Him. By frustrating your attempts to get a job when God finally does give you the favor you need to get work you will look to Him and give Him all the praise.

In creation God set the earth in an orbit around the sun, in the same way life brings us to events and experiences that we have seen before. Have you ever wondered why the same thing keeps happening to you? It may be because that experience is what you need to use in your season of operation. In the same way that our life experiences are in motion, so are our seasons. The earth goes through spring, summer, fall, and winter only to prepare the next year for spring, summer, fall, and winter again. Sometimes God will have you alternate between seasons of preparation and operation because He is moving you from one level to another. Each level requires new and different experiences in order for you to operate to your maximum potential.

Moses was in Egypt for forty years and then in the wilderness forty years operating in his secular purpose before God called him out to operate in his spiritual purpose. Jesus walked the face of the earth for thirty-three years but only three of those years were dedicated to His public ministry. We must understand that most of us will spend more time in preparation than we will in operation. I believe God has ordained this for some of us because He does not want us to lose our focus on Him.

Most of us have never considered the difference between who we are and an apple seed. When an apple seed is planted it knows that it will one day become an apple tree but it does not break through the ground until it has matured. The apple seed will bring forth apples and not oranges because it is obedient to its purpose and timing. For some of us, the apple seed is smarter than we are because the apple seed knows its purpose and many of us do not. Even if we do know our purpose, often we try to bear fruit before our time simply because we do not understand the difference between the season of preparation and the season of operation. Although the apple seed is an inanimate object it is still subject to God as its Creator therefore it responds to what God called it to be and what God called it to do. No matter where we are in life we all need to pray for the obedient sense of purpose and timing of an apple seed.

Our Connection to Others

When we are joined to people who are connected to God and share a common sense of purpose we can benefit from our relationship with them. In 1 Samuel 16:21, we see that David serves Saul as his armor bearer. A distressing spirit has tormented Saul due to his disobedience. David was able to serve Saul by playing music that would comfort him. Here we see that David is able to have a productive relationship with Saul because he was connected to God and his purpose. Throughout David's life, most of his relationship choices are either directly or indirectly related to what God has purposed him to do. In Genesis 2:18, we are told:

> *And the Lord God said it is not good that man should be alone, I will make him a helper comparable to him.*

God created Adam to glorify Him through multiplying on the earth. Adam could not do what God had called him to do by himself therefore He had to give him a helper. In the same way, whatever God has purposed us to do we need help to do it.

I am grateful for God being my source and the purpose for which He has ordained me. I also appreciate the favor He has given me in relationships which have helped me to mold my character and fulfill my purpose. I serve in my local church as the Single Adult Minister. God has used that assignment to show me His favor and keep me focused. Not only has my spiritual purpose drawn me closer to God, I have come to know many wonderful people through the ministry. Where would most of us be without the love and sacrifice of our mothers? Without my mother's efforts I would not have been set up to walk in my calling. While my mother was instrumental in my natural growth, my pastor has made a significant difference in my spiritual growth. I never got to know my natural father but God gave me a spiritual father in my pastor. Much of my success in ministry is due to his influence.

What relationships has God used to impact your life? God did not design us to fulfill our purpose by ourselves. The Body of Christ is a team. In football, two opposing teams compete by using strategies and tactics that are designed to get into the opponent's end zone. One team getting into the other team's end zone accomplishes scoring, which is called a touchdown. Each team is made up of eleven players; each with a different position that is specifically designed for offense or defense. Although the quarterback, offensive backs, and receivers often get the glory for scoring touchdowns, where would they be if the other members of the team were not working in unison? Teamwork is a relationship principle that applies whether we are perfecting our family, ministerial, professional, or personal relationships.

Often times in our Western culture, we think of relationships in terms of romance, marriage, and sex. This simplistic view of relationships sometimes does not allow God to provide us with the help we need in building our character and fulfilling our purpose. The lifeblood of any relationship extends beyond the acknowledgement of God and sharing in a like purpose to the ability to communicate with those you are in relationship with. We will look at three basic components of communication: conversation, connection, and communion. How far you should go in the communication process is going to be directly related to what you discern God's purpose for that relationship.

Conversation

Conversation is communicating by the expression of thoughts and feelings verbally. If a person you are in a relationship with is serving time in the military or in prison, you may choose to communicate with them via letter or e-mail. Written communication is also necessary within our professional relationships but personal relationships are more intimate when the parties talk to one another.

Have you ever had somebody say something to you that made you so angry that you felt like slapping him or her? It's not just what you say and how you say it; it is also when you say it. In your professional relationship with your supervisor, it would be wise to take some time to calm down if you are angry with him or her. Not only is time necessary to cool down tempers but it would also be appropriate to discuss your issues in private so that neither party will be embarrassed. A good rule of thumb is to always commend in public and criticize in private. If you are suspicious of the possible outcome of a private meeting, try to have an objective party sit in to arbitrate, if necessary.

When parents speak with their children, they need to understand that words are like empty containers. If a parent encourages their child saying, "Even though you failed that test, we will get you a tutor." Those words spoken in a soft tone can be like a cold glass of water on a hot day. Conversely, if a parent says, "You will never amount to anything," those words spoken in a harsh tone can be like a warm glass of 80-proof vodka on a Friday night. The point is that our conversation can be refreshing or intoxicating. Is your conversation overly critical? Perhaps there are unresolved issues in your heart that you need to pray and ask God how to deal with. It is important that those heart issues are handled properly not just for our own emotional health but for the emotional health of those who we are in relationships with as well.

Connection

Connection is a form of communication that occurs when people sense they are being joined together through something that they both have in common. When you are connected it is like putting your car in drive, once you are in drive you can move forward once you begin accelerating. Conversely when you are not connected it is like putting your car in park, if you accelerate all you are doing is revving your engine. A relationship without some type of connection is not going anywhere.

God is a triune being. He is the Father, the Son, and the Holy Spirit. He created us in His image, spirit, soul, and body. Members of the same church should connect spirit to spirit with their pastor because he provides godly direction for them. A spiritual connection includes the pastor speaking to some areas in your life he or she could not have known independent of the Holy Spirit. If a church member does not sense a spirit-to-spirit connection, it is possible they are worshipping at the wrong church and they need to seek God's direction and guidance.

Sometimes in the academic environment of undergraduate or graduate school, a teacher and student have a soul-to-soul intellectual connection because of how well the teacher relates the subject matter to the student. Have you ever had a teacher you really liked? It is possible you had an emotional connection where you sensed that the teacher cared. This feeling probably facilitated the learning process and made for a better student-teacher relationship.

Often times people who pledged in the same sorority or fraternity have a sense of connection because of their similar experience. People connect sometimes based on sharing the same socio-economic, cultural, gender, or racial status. These types of connections give the parties involved a common frame of reference that enables them to bond. Sometimes God wants us to stretch emotionally and intellectually by crossing social, cultural, and racial barriers so that we can connect spiritually through Christ-centered relationships. This can make us feel uncomfortable but challenge us to grow.

When a man and a woman find each other physically attractive, there develops a body-to-body connection. Have you ever found yourself gravitating toward people that you find are attractive? If the answer is yes, this may be due to the release of a chemical in the brain called dopamine. This chemical acts like morphine and gives us a sense of intoxication. Our connection to attractive people is sometimes a soul-to-soul connection but more often than not we are chasing the high we get when we are in their company. This is part of the reason that marriages have difficulties after the honeymoon is over. The reality of a day-to-day relationship has a tendency to decrease physical attraction and challenge the couple to connect in other areas. We not only are connected to people who are attractive, but we can also connect to places and things that we find attractive. The reason we feel better when we wear certain clothing or when we are in a place that we like is fundamentally the same reason we feel good about people we are attracted to. It is important that we understand that dopamine has a powerful influence in our lives and it motivates us to want to be connected to some of the people that we care for. In order to maintain a proper balance we need to become more reliant upon our vertical spiritual connection to God than our horizontal connection to others.

Communion

Communion is communication that transcends conversation and connection to a dimension where the people involved simply enjoy spending time in one another's presence. While conversation and connection are necessary for a good relationship to exist between your colleagues, communion is not necessary. If a married teacher seeks to have communion with a student who is single and also a member of the opposite sex, these actions would be questionable. Conversely, communion is very appropriate between parents and children. Families should be able to live in the same house, have family meals, and go on vacations together for the sole purpose of enjoying one another's company.

Friendship is another relationship that is enhanced by communion. Have you ever had a friend who finished your sentences before you could complete them? Perhaps when you were emotionally distraught they knew you so well that they just were silent and kept you company. This type of communion is truly a blessing to all that have experienced it.

Marriage is the most important relationship where communication through communion should exist. Could you imagine what it would be like to be married to someone who you did not enjoy being around? Single people sometimes marry for all the wrong reasons. It could be for sex, money, or just to satisfy their loneliness. If they did not have good conversation, connection, and communion before marriage, it is difficult to establish those things after marriage. For a healthy marriage, both parties need to communicate their likes and dislikes in a loving non-confrontational manner. With much prayer and faith the difficulties of marriage can be overcome.

A relationship without communication is like a plant without water; eventually it will die. God desires to use each of us in our relationships but He cannot use us to the fullest unless we ask Him how to properly communicate with those we are in relationship with.

Summary

David was a man after God's own heart. David was connected to God and he understood God as his source. This relationship gave birth to his purpose. As a result of David walking in purpose, he made relationship choices that were connected to his purpose.

Our most important relationship is our relationship with God because He is our source and the author of all things good. When we are vertically connected to Him, He will reveal to us our purpose and lead us to relationships that help fulfill that purpose. There is a descending priority in relationships that begins with God's purpose and those relationships that are related to that purpose. It is important that we don't get our priorities confused by putting our purpose or intimate relationships ahead of God because this is spiritual idolatry.

It is natural for us to allow our desire for our relationships to precede God and His purpose. Hence if we understand this principle we can make the appropriate modifications in our lives. We risk making erroneous choices in our relationships any time we take our eyes off God and our purpose. It is inevitable that we will face challenges in our relationships. We must remember it is God who allows those challenges to perfect our character and prepare us for our purpose.

CHAPTER TWO

Types of Relationships

-=ЯҌ-

(What lane are you in?)

Have you ever merged into an interstate highway and crossed from your lane to the center lane without looking? Have you ever had another driver change lanes in front of you without signaling? The traffic codes in most states require that a driver maintain their vehicle entirely in one lane of travel unless they are changing lanes. Before changing lanes, it is required that you signal your intentions manually or electronically. Traffic lanes are intended to be boundaries, which are put in place to facilitate the orderly flow of traffic. If traffic lanes were not in place, there would be a great chance for traffic gridlock, which has the potential to lead to accidents.

It is difficult for most of us to see the invisible boundaries that exist in relationships. These boundaries are determined by God's purpose for the relationship and the type of relationship we believe it should be. When we decide to cross the boundaries of our relationships without communicating that intention, it is like changing lanes without putting on your turn signal. Many people have crashed because they did not understand God's purpose for their relationship therefore, they moved from one type to another. When you violate the boundaries of relationships and cross over into the wrong type of relationship, not only is there a potential to crash but you also risk being the source of an emotional gridlock. This emotional gridlock can manifest itself through experiences that could have been avoided had the people involved stayed in their lane. Sometimes people in a professional relationship cross the boundary into a personal relationship and end up not being able to work together due to the inability to handle differences in each type of relationship. Sometimes people in a ministry relationship cross the boundary into a business relationship only to discover that the other person has unethical business practices. Unfortunately, this may jeopardize the initial relationship and lead to contention that could have been avoided. In this chapter, we will look at family, ministry, professional, and personal relationships. We will also examine how to avoid the risks we take when we move from one relationship type to another.

Family Relationships

Our family relationships are with those people who are connected by a common ancestry. They include blood relatives, relatives by marriage, and adopted family members. In 1 Samuel 16:10, we are told that after Samuel arrived in Bethlehem to anoint the next king of Israel, Jesse paraded his oldest sons before the prophet. Samuel rejected them and later chose David as king. Saul was the first king of Israel but he was from the tribe (or family) of Benjamin. It was God's original intention that the royalty of His people would descend from the tribe (or family) of Judah. In the same way that God had a plan for each of the twelve tribes (or families) of Israel, He has a plan for our family.

David was ignored by his father and rejected by his

mother. David's dysfunctional family relationship may have contributed to the contention that would later evolve in his other relationships. It is important to understand that the family is the classroom for future relationships. Social and cultural mores learned at home are likely to be displayed outside of the home. One of the best ways to understand your present is to revisit your past. Our past begins with our family and how we were raised. Unless we look to God to enable us to change, our past will become our future.

When I visited my past, I realized that as a single parent my mother did the best that she could do in raising me. I grew up as an only child with a melancholy introverted temperament. As a young adult, I was selfish and self-centered because I did not know how to interrelate with different types of people. Although my experience with my natural family did not compel me to come out of my box, my spiritual family did. Part of God's purpose for me is to minister to His people. When I began serving in my local church, I found a new family that challenged me to grow. In my case my spiritual family provided much of the maturity and life experience that I should have received within my natural family. In Genesis 12:3, God says to Abraham:

> *I will bless those who bless you, and I will curse those who curse you; and in you all the families of the earth shall be blessed.*

God addressed Abraham because He intended that the primary family member would be the father. The ideal family will have a father and mother in the home. When the father is absent, there are difficulties that are likely to arise because his absence is not according to God's original plan. The way to handle those difficulties is with the wisdom God provides through prayer. When the father is absent the mother has no other choice but to assume the responsibility of headship. The head of household who is obedient to God will not only receive an individual blessing just as He blessed Abraham but those blessings will also be shared with others.

Parents

Have you ever been at the grocery store and saw some rude and disrespectful children? If you ask average public school teachers what was one of the major causes for disruptions in their classes, they would tell you the parents. Parents need to understand that what they do or don't do in the presence of their children will effect what their children do or don't do when they are absent. When parents don't teach their children respect through self-discipline in the home, that lack of self-discipline becomes disrespect outside the home.

Sometimes parents see uniformed police officers in public places and when their children misbehave, they say to the child, "that police officer will lock you up." If you are a parent who has done this, you are in error. The discipline of your children should only occur outside the home when it has failed inside the home. Sometimes parents do not want the responsibility of disciplining their children, which has the potential to lead to spoiled children. Unfortunately, spoiled children have the potential to become rotten adults. Therefore, parents need to understand that their discipline should be given in light of their own self-discipline. Parents who are not self-disciplined appear as hypocrites to their children when they try to correct their children. The parents' motivation for self-discipline is not just because of their relationship with God but because they want the best for their children. Parents who give their children whatever they want whenever they want are not being good examples of self-discipline. As children mature, rewards should be given for good behavior and tangible demonstrations of their being accountable. Good grades and chores completed deserve a reward such as an allowance or some type of privilege that could include extra-curricular activities such as sports or having company.

Parents harm their children by drinking, smoking, and engaging in sexual immorality in the presence of their children. The child's first frame of reference is the parent. Therefore, what you do as a parent has the potential to be emulated by your child. The parent that over eats not only needs to use self-discipline in their eating habits for their own health but there needs to be concern that the child will possibly become an overeater also. We should always want better for our children than we have done for ourselves.

Imagine this: your child comes home from school and you instruct him or her to wash the dishes before he or she goes to bed, he or she responds in a sarcastic tone saying "there were no dishes in the sink when I left!" What would you do? If you are from the "old school" you might try to slap the child into tomorrow. But if you are from the "new school" you might get into an argument with your child despite the fact that he or she does not pay any bills in the house. It is possible that the parents will have different ideas on how to handle this situation. Parents need to come together for the children's sake to represent a united front especially in matters of discipline. Some children are extremely perceptive and have the ability to sense which parent is weaker than the other. In these cases, children can play one parent against another, which is why parents need to be on one accord. This is especially true in the matters of corporal punishment. The decision to discipline a child physically should be mutual when both parents live in the home together. Once the decision is made, corporal punishment should only be administered when the parent who is administering the punishment is not angry. If the child is of age, the reason for the punishment should be explained before it is administered. It is important that the motivation for any type of discipline be love with the ultimate objective of correcting the behavior that is in error. The type of corporal punishment used should not leave bruises or scars. After any type of discipline is administered, there should be a period where the parents affirm their love for the child.

Single Parents

Single parenting is sometimes the result of sexual immorality, divorce, separation, or the death of one parent. The single parent's first priority should be their relationship with God and second their relationship with their children. Some parents allow their career to take precedence over their children. In these situations, there is money for the children but the children are lost because they are not likely to have received the parental guidance needed. Unless there is a significant trust fund involved, the single parent must work to support their family without neglecting their children. This can be accomplished by enlisting the help of friends, members of your natural family, or your church family. Although professional daycare is very expensive, the single parent has to think, "How much is the safety and welfare of my children worth?"

If you are a single parent, you have to give prayerful thought to the importance of a romantic relationship. Romantic relationships for the single parent have the potential to compromise the relationship with the children. This occurs when there is inadequate communication between the adults involved. An individual may get involved in the life of the children, then when there is a problem in the relationship with the parent; the children may suffer if the relationship is abandoned. This is why the partner should not be exposed to the children unless there is a commitment in the relationship to the possibility of marriage. Once trust is established, the partner can begin to build a relationship with the children. If there is a mutual connection between the children and the partner, the two adults should prayerfully consider dating, courtship, and marriage. One way to determine if a single parent is ready to get married is to see how he or she responds to his or her partner's disciplining the children. If the single parent does not trust the judgment of his or her partner, then there is a problem that needs to be resolved before the relationship moves further. This can be accomplished through prayerful communication as well as having an objective party involved who can offer godly counsel.

The single parent may have to sacrifice their interest in romantic relationships especially if the person of interest has no desire to grow with the children. There is no sense in starting something that you cannot finish. The parent and their children are inextricably connected and any romantic relationship with a future must consider this as a "package deal." Although it is possible to develop mature adult relationships apart from the children, the single parent has to consider their own level of spiritual maturity. Ask yourself, "Is this what God wants?" "Should I engage in a relationship that has no emotional future?" "Is this relationship productive or is it a waste of time?" "Am I compromising any standards for temporal companionship and happiness?" Only God can answer these questions within the heart of a single parent.

Siblings

Parents set the atmosphere for how their children interact with one another. Unfortunately, parents sometimes give one child more favored treatment than the others. This not only creates contention between the siblings but it is also the root of jealousy, anger, resentment, and bitterness. No parent is perfect but he or she should make an attempt to love their children equally and keep an open line of communication.

Sibling relationships don't just include biological brothers and sisters but they also include stepchildren. Many marriages will require the blending of two distinctly different groups of people. The adults in these relationships are responsible for finding areas where there are common interests. These areas can include church activities, athletic functions, and eating together at mealtime to foster communication and family harmony.

Parents should encourage their children to take responsibility for one another and be "their brother's keeper." Parents can demonstrate positive and healthy relationships with their own siblings. As the siblings mature, they will have to take responsibility for how close they remain. Sometimes college, the military, and marriage can put distance in the sibling relationship but this is natural and to be expected.

Extended Family Relationships

Our extended family includes all of our family outside the immediate household. The relationship that often poses the greatest threat to a marriage is the "in-laws" or as some might call them the "out laws" if they become the source of contention in the household. In marriage, not only are two distinctly different people coming together joining as one, but also the families of both spouses are in essence uniting as well.

If your son or daughter marries, he or she ceases to have the same level of responsibility and accountability to you as a parent. The day your children exchange vows is the day a new family is begotten. It is inevitable that married life will bring challenges to your children but wisdom says for you to keep your prayers much and your advice little. I recognize this is easier said than done but God can teach them lessons they cannot learn from you. You also owe them a vote of confidence in their maturity. Give them a chance to succeed or fail on their own. Sometimes we can be a crutch to those we love. When you walk with a crutch, you will walk with a limp until you find the strength to walk on your own. Whenever possible, parents need to allow their adult children to walk on their own with the help of God.

There may be times when the marriage has physical, mental, or emotional abuse that needs outside help. Sometimes the weaker spouse will abandon the marriage leaving the other party in financial trouble. Under these circumstances, the family should intercede with spiritual, mental, emotional, and financial support. Perhaps you should provide shelter for your child, if they have been abandoned. Your direct loving support will most likely facilitate the healing that is necessary for them to grow in character. If the challenges that your child faced in the marriage are beyond your ability to give, prayerfully seek ministerial or professional help for your loved ones.

Have you ever seen a momma's boy? He is typically a grown man but he still depends on his mother for those things he should be able to provide for himself. Daddy's girl does basically the same thing as an adult, yet in times of distress, she looks to her father for comfort and security. Adult children must learn to become independent of parental influence once they become married because marriage makes your spouse your primary responsibility next to God. Independence comes by having faith in God and communicating with your spouse. Both of you should make small decisions together and step out on them. As time passes on, you will make bigger and bigger decisions together that should facilitate the marital bond.

Uncles, aunts, and cousins also make up the extended family. How intimate your relationship is with them will depend on the emotional investment they make in your life. If you don't connect with them, it is proper to respect their position in your family but you should not feel any obligation that transcends the conviction of the Holy Spirit within.

Sometimes our ministry relationships will provide more of a sense of purpose and comfort than our family relationships. This is the reason we need to understand the differences in relationships and be willing to grow in them according to God's purpose.

Ministry Relationships

Our ministry relationships are with those people who are connected by serving in the same divine purpose. These relationships include people who are a part of the same church or ministry. In 1 Samuel 18:8, we see that Saul was not happy with David becoming more popular than he. Apparently, David was rejected by his natural father and subsequently adopted by Saul when he went to serve Saul as his armor bearer. David eventually became a captain in Saul's army leading to numerous victories over the Philistines. This gave birth to Saul's jealousy.

David's ministry relationship with Saul illustrates how God will use those relationships not only to make up for the deficiencies in our family relationships but also to build character in other areas of our lives. Everything that David learned in his ministry relationship with Saul prepared him for his future ministry relationships. In 2 Corinthians 5:18, we are told:

> *Now all things are of God, who has recon-*
> *ciled us to Himself through Jesus Christ, and*
> *has given us the ministry of reconciliation.*

Once we accept Jesus Christ as our Lord and Savior, through faith He comes to live inside us through the Holy Spirit. He will lead us to reconcile those who are unsaved to Him. We accomplish this through prayerfully sharing the word of God and our testimony. Sometimes God will use us to reconcile those who are saved because they are dealing with some specific challenge in their lives that God has given us the wisdom to speak to. As a Christian, our primary purpose in relationships is not to have our own personal needs met but to be a light to those who are lost and don't know Christ. We should also be a source of strength and comfort to other Christians.

Can you imagine what it would be like to need extra money? My adult experience with ministry relationships began at my local church in response to my desire to supplement my income. I was drawn to my church by a part-time job opportunity to direct traffic on Sunday mornings. My church needed uniformed police officers to work off duty during the times we had service. One Sunday morning after all the traffic had died down; I decided to sit outside in front of the sanctuary. While sitting there I heard this loud, powerful voice emanating from inside the sanctuary. That was the voice of the pastor who would later become my spiritual father in the ministry. At that time, my church had no ministry for single adults and one thing led to another and I helped to establish the Single Adult Ministry. After I received my call to the ministry, I later received my ministry license and after that I was ordained and elevated to the office of church elder. As I mentioned before, my temperament is that of an introverted melancholy. Not only am I an introvert but I was also raised as an only child. My serving in ministry has forced me to mature in ways that would have probably been neglected apart from the relationships that I have encountered in my ministry service.

God intends for the local church to be governed theocratically. This means that God appoints an individual to be the leader and visionary for that local body. Many churches are governed democratically. This means that a group of people who have been elected to administrate the affairs of the church or the congregation, votes on church matters. Democratic government is the best form of civil government because there is a system of checks and balances that aide in overcoming the abuse of authority. Democratic government also gives the people it serves a voice in their government. Many churches have been successful with democratic government but we need to be careful about taking the secular principle of democracy and bringing it into God's church, which is intended to be spiritual. Although democracy in the church may be the people's choice, it is not God's choice. Whether it's the theocratic leadership of Moses in the Old Testament or of Paul in the New Testament, the Bible makes clear God's preference in church government is theocracy.

With this in mind the leadership and members of the church that accepts God's theocratic government should rally around the vision of the set man or woman and help it come to pass. The set man or woman is the pastor or ministry leader that finds themselves in that position through the sovereignty of God. The common sense of purpose and direction creates a sense of family and belonging. The senior pastor of the local church also serves as a type of spiritual father. God intends for a natural father in the family relationship to carry the bulk of the responsibility for the family. In the same way that he is ultimately accountable to God, so is the spiritual father ultimately accountable for the spiritual family God has made him steward over. Wisdom dictates that a spiritual father will have other mature men and women that he can rely on to help him do what God called him to do but he understands he will ultimately give an account to God. When a church is being led by the Holy Spirit and governed by godly men and women who use biblical standards for leadership and service, it becomes a place where the members can grow in the Lord.

Cults

Do you think the senior pastor should have the final say

in matters of church government? Many people say no because they believe that absolute power corrupts absolutely. Our recent history has shown how cult leaders abuse the ministerial relationship with their followers to serve their own selfish agenda. A cult is a religious sect that is viewed as illegitimate by mainstream orthodox faiths.

On November 18, 1978, Jim Jones ordered his People's Temple cult followers to commit mass suicide in Jonestown, Guiana. He was alleged to have emotionally, sexually, and physically abused members of his group. An estimated 918 people ended their lives by drinking Kool-Aid laced with cyanide.

On April 19, 1993, David Koresh ordered his Branch Davidian cult followers to resist Federal agents who were attempting to serve arrest warrants on him for weapons charges. It was also alleged that he had emotionally, sexually, and physically abused members of his group. The stand-off in Waco, Texas lasted 51 days. After the standoff ended, 74 of his followers were dead along with 4 Federal agents. It is suspected that his followers set the fire inside the compound that facilitated the end of the standoff.

On March 27, 1997, Marshal Apperwhite ordered his Heaven's Gate cult followers to commit suicide by consuming poison. He and 30 of his San Diego, California members believed that in death they would be caught up in a UFO that was traveling behind the comet Hale Bopp.

Ministry relationships are different from family relationships because you get to choose whether you want to become a part of a ministry unlike the family you were born or adopted into. Anytime we have a choice there is a responsibility that comes with that choice.

In most cults, the focus is generally more on the leader or a specific doctrine than God. Sometimes cult members are estranged from their natural family and turn to the cult as their spiritual family. This is the reason why the home is the primary place to build a foundation for positive and healthy relationships. Even though there may have been some deficiency in the family life of the adult cult member, they still share some of the responsibility for their actions. God will ultimately judge the cult leader who has misled their followers but many cult members voluntarily submit to their ungodly spiritual authority.

We must seek God in prayer about our participation in any ministry along with searching the scriptures ourselves in order to discern if what is being taught is true. We are not only responsible for ourselves but also for our loved ones who are within our sphere of influence. We should pray for them and offer sound biblical counsel as long as they will listen. For those who insist on going the way of the cult despite our best efforts, we have to trust that God has a plan that transcends our understanding.

Spiritual Authority

Who do you respect more your pastor/ministry leader or your supervisor at work? Many people respect their secular leadership at work more than their spiritual leadership at church. Sometimes this is because those who are in spiritual authority have abused that authority. Most of us are more concerned about the natural bread we earn over the spiritual bread that is given to us by those who are in spiritual authority. The truth of the matter is that our pastor and his or her church leadership represent the spiritual authority that God desires to use to mature our character and help us reach our destiny. The reward we get from submitting to their lawful authority is eternal. Conversely the reward we get from submitting to the lawful authority of secular leadership is temporal.

Changing churches is generally easier than changing jobs because for most of us our career is not connected to the church. Sometimes church growth is based more on rotation than multiplication. By this I mean that church members rotate from one church to another because they do not wish to submit to spiritual authority. In this situation, there is no true multiplication of new converts just people going from one church to another. This is not to say that the pastor or church leadership is perfect but God allows the human frailties of some to expose the human frailties of others. You may feel as if what is going on in your church is not fair, and while this may be true God is more concerned about using life's experiences to teach you faithfulness than what we perceive is fair. We live in what I call a "quit society". We quit not only our jobs and marriages but also our churches. The problem is if you can't handle where you are it will be equally difficult for you to handle where you are going. Unfortunately, when we quit our churches prematurely, we do not give God the opportunity to finish the work He started in us.

If your church leadership is morally, legally, or ethically corrupt, separating yourself from that church may be reasonable and prudent. But if you are convinced that you were led to that church or ministry by God and your flesh tells you to leave because you are uncomfortable, perhaps God is using that ministry relationship to teach you humility and build your character.

Not only does the churches lay membership sometimes change like the wind but sometimes church leadership does also. At times, this is due to the church member or leader being more connected to the soul of the pastor rather than the spirit of the pastor. We can know if we are connected to the soul of our pastor if they fail to return our telephone call or neglect us in some way and we leave the church simply because we are offended. If we have a selfish agenda in being a part of a ministry and that selfish agenda does not come to pass it is likely we will be disappointed in our soul. That disappointment may lead to our leaving the church.

Perhaps the church member or church leader who is connected to the spirit of their pastor may discern the reason that the pastor did not speak when he or she walked by them is because they were preoccupied with a church crisis or their own personal problem. A mature church member or church leader understands that their pastor may be emotionally available Monday and be emotionally unavailable Tuesday all because they are trying to handle the weight of the ministry. We need to honestly ask ourselves "am I connected to the soul or spirit of my pastor?"

On occasion the spiritual sons and daughters of a ministry who serve in church leadership become disappointed when their spiritual gifts are not recognized. Those who have been called to preach and teach may get disappointed when their pastor does not give them the opportunity to minister the word on Sunday morning. It should be understood that the primary voice to the local congregation is the voice of the senior pastor. It is his or her responsibility to hear from God and provide leadership to the flock that he or she has been given stewardship over. The person who is called to preach or teach under their pastor should ask God to give them opportunities within the local church to teach Bible classes and serve wherever they are needed. They should also use the season of what appears to be nothingness to develop their ministry management skills by taking small ministry projects and carrying them to completeness. God will also open doors to minister the word outside the local church. If God calls someone to preach or teach He opens doors for them to do what He has called them to do.

Another challenge we sometimes face is the pastor/spiritual leader may be so occupied with other matters that his or her neglect may be perceived as a deliberate offense. Under these circumstances it is easy to think to yourself "I will go where I am celebrated not stay where I am tolerated." If the church leader leaves the church with this attitude their motive is probably born out of selfishness and changing churches will only spread that selfishness to another church body. Church leadership and laity alike need to understand that "it is not about us," it is about fulfilling the call of God on your life and advancing the vision of the senior pastor. If you believe that the ministry you are serving in is outside the call of God on your life or you do not believe in the vision of the senior pastor then I recommend that after you have prayed and sought the will of God in the matter that you speak with your pastor before making your final decision.

Sometimes God is using our ministry relationships that make us feel uncomfortable to teach us commitment and faithfulness because one day we will occupy that same or greater place of authority. We should ask God if we need to change our attitude before we change our church. If you have peace with God about changing churches, then you should try to meet with your pastor so that both of you may get closure. If he or she is unavailable for you to meet with them, you should attempt to speak with a member of church leadership or you may write a letter informing the church staff of your decision. This should be done not just for closure but also as a courtesy to those who are in spiritual authority.

The Spirit of Servanthood

Perhaps you are thinking, "what do I say to the person who says I don't need to go to church to worship God?" This is true, but there is a difference between our individual worship time with God at home and our corporate worship time with a group of believers who share the same sense of purpose. The difference is the sense of unity and family that reveals another dimension of God. Another reason regular church attendance is important is because it puts us in a position to develop ministry relationships and to serve God. Through our willingness to serve God we not only can be a blessing to others but our character will be strengthened.

Have you ever felt that your local church was like a nightclub? Large urban churches draw all kinds of people from all walks of life. Small rural churches are like families with a unique set of challenges all their own. Many people have different agendas for why they are attending church. Some people want to network for business opportunities and some people tired of the club scene want to meet a nice member of the opposite sex who is a Christian. Whatever the motive for a ministry relationship, your motive should be to serve God by ministering to people in a way the pastor cannot. If you are involved in a ministry activity and someone passes you a business card or attempts to flirt with you, try asking them the following questions:

- *If you were to rate your relationship with God on a scale of 1 to 10, where would you stand?*
- *What is the last thing God revealed to you in prayer?*
- *What did you get out of the sermon today and how did it relate to you?*

By asking these questions you have just changed the focus of the person's interest from horizontal (whatever their interest was in you) to vertical (what God desires for the relationship to be). How you proceed from that point is going to depend on your personal conviction and what you discern God desires to do through that relationship.

Many people attend church to hear the preacher or to listen to the choir. If that is your intention, in essence you are like a spectator who goes to their favorite athletic event or concert. Sunday morning for many is a spiritual form of entertainment when it should be an opportunity to serve. The person you are sitting next to may need a meal or a ride home but we are so busy being a spectator in the stands that we miss the opportunity to play in the field. We should pray that God not only gives us a word on Sunday morning but that He gives us an opportunity to serve Him by ministering to His people.

Traditionally twenty percent of the people in church do eighty percent of the work. Most churches cannot afford to pay for everything they need; therefore, if you have some area of expertise and you have the time to donate to the church, please ask God to give you the opportunity to do so. You will find your strengths and weaknesses when you begin working for no pay. There will be those people that you serve within ministry that you will question their salvation. There will be others that you will grow closer to than your own family. If there is not an opportunity to serve in your local church, you can also ask God to lead you to a civic group that can use your gifts, talents, and abilities. Serving in the local church can be one of the most rewarding experiences you will ever have but you do not want to serve to the exclusion of your other responsibilities. If a husband needs to be at his sons football practice then he needs to put family first. Likewise a wife does not need to neglect her husband in order to be at every church meeting. The key word here is "balance." If necessary we need to set a schedule so that we do not neglect any of our adult responsibilities.

If your interest in a family member takes on a spiritual emphasis through prayer and sharing wisdom from the word of God, that family relationship becomes a ministry relationship. The same is true if you develop a spiritual connection with a colleague at work because of a personal dilemma he or she is going through; the professional relationship becomes a ministry relationship. A word of caution, you never want to force your faith on another person but you always want to be in a position to speak the truth in love. Our ministry relationships are one of the primary means

God wants to use to build character in us and be a blessing to His people.

Professional Relationships

Our professional relationships are with those people who are connected by working or by doing business together. In 1 Samuel 28:2, we see that the Philistine King Achish used David in a professional capacity as one of his bodyguards. During this time, David left the service of Saul because of Saul's attempts to kill him. Saul not only had a ministry relationship with David as one of his spiritual sons but he also had a professional relationship with him since David was one of the captains of his army. Saul's disobedience made him vulnerable to a depressing spirit that altered his perspective on everything around him. Therefore, Saul perceived that David was his enemy, which forced David to seek employment elsewhere. In Colossians 3:17, we are told:

> *And whatever you do in word or deed, do all*
> *in the name of the Lord Jesus, giving thanks*
> *to God the father through Him.*

God is not only involved in our family and ministry relationships, He is also involved in everything we do which includes our professional relationships. We need to be mindful that our actions at work and with those that we do business with reflect our faith in God. If we keep this in mind this will help us walk in integrity in our professional relationships.

Police uniforms are generally comprised of a man's shirt, pants, and shoes. Most police departments require that female officers either wear their hair short or pinned up and the use of makeup is discouraged. These factors sometimes make female officers appear to be physically unattractive. On one occasion, I saw one of my female colleagues out of uniform and I could not believe my eyes. Her hair was down and she was wearing a tight top and snug blue jeans. She looked ten times better than she did in uniform. I can honestly say that this woman looked like a movie star. Although, I can recall being very attracted to her, I was convicted that I should not pursue a personal relationship with her because of our professional relationship. Several years later, I got promoted and I became one of her supervisors. I never told her of my attraction to her because I did not want to compromise the integrity of our professional relationship. I believe my ability to supervise her may have been compromised had we had a personal relationship. I have made many mistakes in relationships but I was excited that this time I listened to that still, small voice of the Holy Spirit.

In our professional relationships we must ask ourselves if our conduct is immoral, illegal, or unethical.

Immoral Conduct

Have you ever heard a rumor about married colleagues at work having an affair? If the rumor is true, this conduct is considered immoral. Morals are maximum standards of behavior that have biblical truth as their foundation. Examples of immoral conduct include sexual immorality, lying, and stealing. If your supervisor gives you an assignment and you forget to complete it, you should be honest when asked about the assignment. If you lie and say you completed it, you must realize that the consequences of the lie are likely to be greater than the consequences of the truth. Lying compounds the problem because if your lie is uncovered you not only have to face the inefficiency of not completing your assignment but you also have to face the assault on your integrity. Trust is an invaluable commodity in the workplace that you do not want to forfeit. If you are wrong, admit your error. Trust God to give you grace and mercy and commit yourself to do better.

Do you know someone who has taken office supplies from work for their own personal use? Perhaps you use the copier at work for personal use without the permission of your supervisor. Although this may seem petty, these actions are immoral because technically they are stealing. Have you ever called in sick when you were not? This too is immoral because the action is based on a lie. Most of the time these practices are common place but the Christian must always be aware of how immoral conduct has the potential to compromise their ability to minister to their colleagues. Perhaps you are saying "it can't be wrong because everyone is doing it." This is not true. There are many people who walk in integrity. Although we know that no one is perfect we should not make excuses for our character flaws when it is in our power to do the right thing.

Illegal Conduct

Being discriminated against based on race, religion, sex, or national origin is considered to be illegal. If an action is considered illegal it is contrary to federal, state, or local statutes and may be punishable by a fine, imprisonment, or both. All mankind is a part of God's creation. Therefore, we are all equal in essence. If a person does not get a job, promotion, transfer or any other professional benefit, it should be due to the lack of experience, skill, or ability and not due to a person's race, religion, sex, or national origin. If you have the authority in the workplace to ensure fair treatment, I admonish you to do so. Failure to act in the case of illegal activity could possibly make you a party to the activity. If you are in a position to help someone who has been discriminated against, that relationship is likely to be a blessing to all parties. Not only might you gain the favor of those you help but you may also be able to save your company from criminal and civil penalties if the illegal activity is discontinued.

If you are a victim of illegal conduct at work, attempt to

address the matter with your supervisor first. If there is a standard operating procedure in your company for handling the matter, you need to follow that procedure. If you are not satisfied with your administrative attempts to resolve the issue, you should report the incident to the police. If in your opinion the incident is grave enough to warrant some type of legal action, ask God to give you the grace to pursue the matter to its end without any malice or bitterness in your heart. If you continue to work during the resolution of the matter, have the attitude that you are going to give your work the best you have to give despite what you are going through. During this process, it would be wise for you to seek the counsel of someone who can be objective. This person can be an attorney or anyone who has professional expertise in the area you are being challenged.

Unethical Conduct

Ethics are standards of behavior that are specifically relevant to a specific profession. If a person is deliberately unproductive at work because he or she is trying to make their supervisor look bad, his or her actions may not be immoral or illegal but they are unethical. If that same supervisor deliberately neglects to confront the inefficiency of that person their actions are considered unethical as well.

Sometimes people play office politics where they deliberately omit important information that needs to be communicated. This may be done to give one group of employees an advantage over another group of employees. Unfortunately, petty people often play the petty game of information starvation. The fact that the act is done deliberately makes it unethical. If you have a colleague that smiles in your face but won't tell you everything you need to know to do your job that tells you where their heart is. It is important to know that people may doubt what you say but they will believe what you do. Whatever negative unethical behavior we see at work we should not repeat it just because that is the status quo. As Christians, our light cannot shine if we do everything that everyone else does. We must remember that we don't just work for pay; we work to make a difference and be an example of integrity.

Sometimes you may unintentionally violate a rule, procedure, or practice. As long as your heart is pure and you are acting in good faith, you will have peace with God. After you have found peace with God, be honest with your supervisor about the matter and make a personal commitment to do better.

Much of our interpersonal conduct at work is not as simple to determine if it is immoral, illegal, or unethical. Therefore, it is incumbent on us to maintain a spirit of meekness not only at work but also in every area of our lives. The more humble we become the easier it will be for us to discern how we should conduct ourselves in our professional relationships.

Personal Relationships

Our personal relationships are with those people who we choose to be socially intimate with. These include friendship, romantic, and marriage relationships. In 1 Chronicles 3:1, we are told about David's six wives and the sons born to him. While David was on the run from Saul, he came in contact with multiple women who he chose to have personal relationships with and marry. Although God warned the kings of Israel not to take multiple wives, David entertained personal relationships with women he should have strictly maintained ministry and professional relationships with. David became selfish and put his agenda ahead of God's agenda. David's error was at the root of much of the strife and contention in his household later in life. In Psalms 139:23-24, we are told:

*Search me O God and know my heart; try me
and know my anxieties; and see if there is
any wicked way in me, and lead me in the
way everlasting.*

We should always ask God to search our heart for the
purpose of uncovering any hidden motives. Sometimes our
conscious motives are good for pursuing a relationship but
subconsciously we may have a hidden agenda that has the
potential of sabotaging the relationship in the future. If our
hidden agendas are exposed to us, God can help us deal with
those issues in private without having to bring unnecessary
emotional baggage to others.

My ex-wife and I served together in the Single Adult
Ministry before we got married. Several years after our
divorce we spoke and I found myself ministering to her in
reference to some challenges she was facing. It occurred to
me that like David, I allowed what should have been a
ministry relationship to become personal, which later caused
both my ex-wife and me a great deal of grief. I have since
learned to ask God to search my heart as to my motive for
wanting to get involved in a personal relationship with an
individual. I have also learned not to cross the line between
ministry and personal relationships without first discerning
the purpose and timing of the relationship. I do not wish to
put God in a box, nor am I saying that a ministry relationship
cannot evolve into a personal relationship but both parties
should consider their level of maturity in handling potential
complications. Understanding God's purpose will determine
whether the relationship should be personal or not. As a
result of my experience I now minister in this area of relationships with understanding because of my past mistakes.

Relationship Pressure

It is natural for a parent to feel pressure to have a

personal relationship with their adult children. Sometimes this can be complicated especially when the child is married with children. The spouse of the child may perceive the parent's personal interest as a violation of their marital space, which in turn may create unnecessary tension in the marriage. Parents need to understand that there are issues that their children will face that only God can resolve. In these situations, not only should the parent be in prayer but also they should let their children know that they will make themselves available for them if they ever need them. After the parent has shared their love with the child, they should respect their space and not intrude unless they are invited.

It is natural for a church member to feel the pressure to want to have a personal relationship with their pastor or the ministry leader that they respect the most. These ministry relationships often have a spirit-to-spirit connection, which has the potential to create a desire to allow the relationship to evolve outside the church. If the church member is lonely or going through some spiritual or emotional crisis, they may reach out to the ministry leader in a personal way and get upset if the ministry leader insists on maintaining a simple ministry relationship. The church member needs to be mature enough to understand that ministry service requires the ministry leader to make priorities. Sometimes family or other responsibilities will not allow the ministry leader to take the relationship outside of the church.

On the other hand, the ministry leader in crisis may reach out for a personal relationship with the church member if they have similar areas of vulnerability. Personal relationships require a degree of emotional intimacy that either person may or may not have the ability to handle. Any individual or shared immaturity has the potential to undermine the good that has been accomplished in the ministry relationship. Before we consider transcending the invisible boundary of the personal and ministry relationship, both people involved should pray and ask God to reveal to them His will for the relationship. If either person does not sense peace in the personal relationship, they should not go forward. If the people have gone forward and found they were in error, they should discuss how they plan to retreat back to the simplicity of the ministry relationship. If feelings are hurt there might be a tendency to abandon the relationship altogether but if possible there should be special attention in salvaging the original purpose for the relationship.

When the leadership component is missing from the ministry relationship the transition to the personal relationship is less complicated. This is true because sometimes we are not as mature as we would like to think we are in terms of handling the personal details of those who are in authority. Those who are in authority have strengths and weaknesses just like any one else. Sometimes when weaknesses of character are exposed it has the potential to undermine the leadership ability of the person who is in authority. The best case scenario for those who are mature is that they may be inclined to support those who are in authority once their weaknesses are exposed. If both parties believe that getting personal is mutually beneficial, then they should prayerfully proceed in faith that God will show Himself faithful in the midst of the relationship.

It is natural for professional colleagues to desire a personal relationship with one another when they connect in areas outside of work. Sometimes colleagues share things in common such as their faith, hobbies, or parenting children. As long as the people involved have enough wisdom not to allow their personal relationship to conflict with their efficiency at work, the relationship has the potential to be a blessing.

If the professional relationship is between a supervisor and subordinate there are ethical questions to consider before getting involved in a personal relationship. The military prohibits fraternization between officers and enlisted personnel. The Officer Corps is the leadership of the military and the enlisted personnel are the followers. It is believed that social fraternization between them has the potential to compromise the officer's ability to lead. Have you ever heard of the saying "familiarity breeds contempt?" Officers can become so friendly with enlisted personnel that in the heat of battle that the enlisted personnel will not take them seriously which may lead to the disobedience of lawful orders. In civilian life, the separation between those who lead and those who follow is not as strict but the principle remains the same. Personal relationships between professional colleagues who have the superior subordinate component can only be successful if the people involved are mature enough to keep the two relationships separate.

Relationship Obligation

Have you ever had a fellow church member or colleague get upset with you because you did not want a personal relationship with them? At no point are you obligated to get personally involved with anyone that you do not have peace with. Sitting next to someone at church or working on a project at work in and of itself does not qualify someone to come into your home have dinner and share the intimate details of your life. People have a myriad of reasons for wanting to get personal with us. Those reasons could be immoral, illegal or unethical. This is the reason the Holy Spirit is invaluable to our decision making process in relationships. We must rely on His still soft voice not only in our relationship choices but in everything that we do. For the individual who has not matured enough spiritually to discern the Holy Spirit's voice, they should look for peace in that person's presence, if peace is absent that is a good sign that something is amiss and that there is a need to seek God further in the matter.

Sometimes people desire to have personal relationships with us because they believe we have the ability to meet some unmet need. Most people have a mental picture of what they desire a relationship to be like, I call this our "relationship paradigm." Our "relationship paradigm" is formulated in our imagination and does not always line up with the will of God. Our "relationship paradigm" may be rooted in our favorite love song or movie character that when we meditate on it long enough it becomes our reality. Then when we perceive that someone is close to our "relationship paradigm" we project our desires onto the other person. Unfortunately we sometimes get upset when the person does not respond the way we would like them to. It should be understood that in our personal relationships we are not obligated to respond to another persons "relationship paradigm." It is important to understand that those persons that we desire to have personal relationships with are not obligated to respond to our "relationship paradigm." We are only obligated to respond personally to those people we believe God has led us to and those people we have already established a personal relationship with such as our friends and of course our mates for those who are married.

God commands that we love one another unconditionally. This means that we are to have His attitude of patience and kindness toward believers and nonbelievers alike. We are to be like God in our demonstration of unconditional love but also like Him in dealing with people differently. God dealt with Saul with judgment as a result of his disobedience but when David sinned against God He dealt with him with grace and mercy after David repented. God dealt with Saul and David differently not just because they had a different heart toward Him but also because He had a different purpose for them. In the same way, we should seek God in prayer as to what His purpose is for that person in our lives. Only after we have peace that part of their purpose is to have a personal relationship with us should we be inclined to allow the relationship to grow more personal.

The Spirit of Fraternity

Why would a college freshman allow himself/herself to be beaten with a paddle until they drew blood? Or worse yet why would they consume alcohol until they were unconscious just to become a member of a fraternity or sorority? This type of activity is considered to be hazing. Hazing is a form of initiation and right of passage in many fraternal organizations. The spirit of fraternity is rooted in our social nature that compels us to want to belong to a group of people even when it has the potential to jeopardize our own health.

The essence of the organized crime of the Italian Mafia and the urban crime of street gangs is the spirit of fraternity. There are people who will risk getting involved in criminal activity and the potential of going to jail simply to have the personal relationships they will enjoy from that specific group. We long for personal relationships and we will connect with groups that we most identify with. Some people play sports not because of their athletic ability but because of an innate desire for the spirit of fraternity. Everyone who joins the military is not patriotic. Some people enlist because the camaraderie and discipline meet their need for personal relationships.

The spirit of fraternity is rooted in our personal need for relationships that may not be met through our family, ministry, or professional relationships. Our primary relationship after God should be our family but sometimes the family unit is so dysfunctional that we meet our relationship needs in other areas. As long as we keep God first and seek relationships that line up with our purpose we are headed in the right direction. We also need to guard against meeting our relationship needs through engaging in immoral, illegal, or unethical conduct. If we keep this principle in mind, we will be at peace with God.

Summary

David's life gives us a panoramic view of family, ministry, professional, and personal types of relationships. David's dysfunctional family relationship with his father and brothers led to his ministry relationship with Saul. Saul became David's spiritual father and both parties were blessed by their relationship. Due to Saul's disobedience, jealousy entered their relationship and David had to separate himself for fear of his life. During this time, David lost focus on God and the purpose for his relationships. This led to a professional relationship with the Philistine king Achish. He later had personal relationships with women that led to multiple marriages. David's life is an example of how if we lose focus on God one bad relationship choice can lead to crossing the boundaries of other relationships that are outside the will of God for our lives.

If we do not understand the difference between family, ministry, professional, and personal relationships, we risk stepping outside the will of God by crossing over the boundaries of those relationships. The choice to move from one relationship to another is not just based on God's will but also what we believe God's purpose is for the relationship. Just because you get along well in your ministry or professional relationship does not mean you will be effective in a personal relationship and vice versa. Even when we keep God first, we may cross over into relationships that we are not emotionally prepared for. As long as we stay humble with our vertical focus on God and keep an open line of communication with those we are in relationship with, we will be able to learn from our mistakes and God will ultimately get the glory.

CHAPTER THREE

Stages of Relationships

❈

(Going from level to level in relationships)

When a woman has a healthy pregnancy she goes through three stages called trimesters. The first twelve weeks of pregnancy is considered the first trimester. During this period the child is considered to be an embryo because its major organs have not developed. The next thirteen weeks is considered the second trimester. During this period the child is no longer considered to be an embryo because the major organs have developed and now the child is called a fetus. The second trimester includes the development of the muscles of the fetus. The last fifteen weeks of pregnancy is considered to be the third trimester. During this period the fetus only has a fifty percent chance of survival outside of the mother's womb because the last stage is necessary for the final development of the fetus.

In life we all go through a standard set of stages: from infancy to toddler; from early childhood to adolescence; from young adulthood to late adulthood. Although there are times we may wish that we could bypass certain stages we must realize that to do so presents a risk, because each stage represents a process that is necessary for us to grow and develop into healthy human beings.

Have you ever been disappointed in one of your relationships? In the same way that a woman's pregnancy has stages that are necessary to the development of her child, personal relationships have stages that are necessary to their healthy development. In this chapter, we will review the stages of relationships. The four basic stages of relationships are stranger, casual acquaintance, intimate acquaintance, and friendship. When you first meet someone, they are a stranger. If during that meeting you connected with similar life experiences and good conversation, does that make them your friend? The answer is no because the relationship has had insufficient time to develop. Oftentimes a person will prematurely identify people they like as friends and they feel betrayed when the relationship fails. Our personal relationships should develop according to the will of God in His timing. Regardless as to whether you are single or married it is important to understand the stages of relationships. If you are married it is likely you will develop other personal relationships outside that of your spouse in which case it is important to allow those relationships to develop according to the will of God. God has a plan for all relationships that He ordains. We need to be prayerful and discerning as to whether we should move from one stage to the next. Our personal relationships are at risk of failure if we do not allow them the proper time to develop.

The Stranger

People who are unknown to us are considered to be strangers. In 1 Samuel 16:6 we are told that Samuel was preparing to anoint David's older brother Eliab as the next King of Israel. Not only did God reject Eliab, He also rejected David's other brothers. Samuel asked David's father, Jesse, if he had any other sons. Jesse sent for David who was tending his sheep. Upon confirmation from the Lord, Samuel anointed David as the next King of Israel. One of the reasons David was initially overlooked by Samuel is because he was a stranger to him. In Hebrews 13:2, we are told:

> *Do not forget to entertain strangers for by so doing some have unwittingly entertained angels.*

We must be careful how we interact with strangers because we never know who they really are. It is possible that the homeless person we walk by could be a messenger from God. Perhaps while Samuel was traveling to Bethlehem he walked by David because he was a stranger and did not realize that he would later anoint him as King.

When I was in the police academy, all of my classmates were strangers to me. Although we were all police recruits, we were not all the same. I can recall one of my classmates who had a very humble spirit who often studied his Bible during our breaks. He later left the police department and became the Minister of Christian Education at my church. While serving in the Single Adult Ministry I became directly accountable to him. He not only became one of my mentors as I matured in ministry, he also provided spiritual covering for me after my marriage failed. My relationship with him taught me a very valuable lesson that a stranger today might become your friend tomorrow.

A stranger is a person who is unknown to you. Although you may not be acquainted in the natural it is possible for the Holy Spirit to give you a sense of peace when in the company of a stranger. In the same way, the Holy Spirit may make us uncomfortable around other strangers as an indication that we do not need to get acquainted with that individual. We should always pray that God reveal to us the difference between the personality, character, and reputation of those we are contemplating a relationship with.

Personality

Have you ever met a stranger and thought to yourself they are really a nice person? But how do you know if they are a nice person if they are a stranger and you just met them? More than likely what you were probably attracted to was the individual's personality. Our personality is the conscious self that we choose to display in public. If you walked into an Army recruiter's office he or she would probably greet you with a smile. The tone in their voice would be warm and friendly. But if you met that same recruiter as a recruit in basic military training they would not greet you with a smile and their tone of voice would be loud and confrontational. Most people display the personality they believe is appropriate for that situation. Since our personality can change at a whim it is not a true indicator of who an individual really is.

Personality is superficial like a beautiful coat of black paint on your favorite sports car. What if you were to look under the hood of that car and find no engine? Can you imagine what it would be like to have a beautiful car that would not start? Personality can be like that sports car with a few rust spots and dings in the body but with a brand new engine. Most of us would rather have a car that runs well rather than a car that looks good. Likewise although personality is important, ultimately the individual's inward character is more important.

Sometimes when we meet strangers we are impressed with their outward pleasant personality. Since we like his or her personality we conclude that the individual is someone we would like to get to know better. In the process of getting acquainted, you may discover that the person is weak in character, almost like the beautiful black sports car with no engine. When we meet strangers we need to understand that there is a distinct difference between personality and character.

Character

Most of us have met someone who appeared to be nice on the surface only to discover that deep within they had issues (like the missing parts in the engine of your favorite car). Character is the subconscious self that we become over a period of time. It is the true person that extends beyond an individual's personality. Therefore, if a person is a stranger to you the only way to get to know their character is by communicating and spending time with one another.

Character in and of it self is neither positive nor negative. If a child grows up in a single parent household with a parent who has neglected them, this will likely have a negative impact on the child's character as an adult. The child's past could possibly contribute to their excessive desire for the clothes and shoes they had to do without as a child. Alternatively, if the same child grows up in a two-parent household where the child's emotional, physical, and financial well-being has been well taken care of it is likely to have a positive impact on the child's character as an adult. The child's past in this situation could possibly contribute to the desire to raise their children in the same manner when they become adults.

The activities we observe in a stranger in the light are likely to be a manifestation of their personality. The activities we observe in that same person in the dark are likely to be their character. Not only is character revealed in the dark behind closed doors but it is also revealed in time. This is the reason that God has us endure a season of preparation before He graces us to operate in the fullness of our divine purpose. It is God's intention that delays in the manifestation of the promises in our lives are intended to build our strength of character. It is important to understand that we have to go beyond the stranger stage of relationships before we can get to know the character of an individual.

Reputation

Have you ever had an opinion about someone based on rumors you've heard from other people? If the answer is yes your opinion is based on that person's reputation. Reputation is different from character because it is what other people say about you, which may not necessarily be who you are. Sometimes people form impressions of strangers based on superficial observations such as what the person is wearing. Although an individual may regularly wear clothing one or two sizes too small this may be more of a manifestation of the person's personality than their character. If multiple people make the same observation the person in question could develop a reputation for being promiscuous without anyone ever taking the time to know their character.

The idea that a stranger is unknown to us should cause us to be neutral in our judgment of them. The reputation of a person is tainted either positively or negatively by the opinions of people who may or may not know the individual's personality or character. Therefore, we should reserve our opinions about strangers until such time as we get acquainted with them.

Casual Acquaintance

A casual acquaintance is a person you know informally. This is a person that you may or may not socialize with. In 1 Samuel 18:1, we are told that Jonathan loved David as himself. Jonathan was Saul's oldest son, which would have made him heir to the throne. David was a stranger to Jonathan and Saul until the battle with the Philistine giant, Goliath.

After David's victory over Goliath his reputation spread throughout all of Israel. After entering Saul's service he became acquainted with Jonathan. The Bible says in Matthew 12:34-35:

> *For out of the abundance of the heart the mouth speaks. A good man out of the good treasure of his heart brings forth good things, and an evil man out of the evil treasure brings forth evil things.*

Although it is possible to mask a deceptive heart with flowery conversation most people over time will reveal their true character in what they say. No matter how much we love the Lord it is inevitable that under the right set of circumstances we will say something that does not magnify God. What reveals the true heart is what we say on a consistent basis in both public and private. It is critical for us to understand that importance of communication if we desire to move from the stranger to the casual acquaintance stage of relationships.

I am grateful for the biblical teaching gift that God has given me. Like any good teacher I am concerned that my students grasp as much of the lessons as possible. In order to insure that my students are learning, I instituted a system where if they have a personal computer with Internet access they can send me their homework on-line. I sometimes offer comments on their homework assignments and answer any questions that may arise. Over the years this system has developed into a very effective tool to develop my ministry relationships. On one occasion, one of my sisters in Christ began e-mailing me in response to the Bible studies. Suddenly her e-mails turned from being ministry focused into being personally focused. I was offended by the individual's comments because she spoke as if she knew me but we had never met. I felt her personal comments were inappropriate because the reason I gave my e-mail address to my students was to facilitate my ministry relationships not establish personal relationships. After steaming over her comments, I sought the Lord in the matter. When I calmed down God showed me that the ministry was more important than my bruised ego and that humility was more important than being right. It also occurred to me that her e-mails were missing one of the most important elements of communication, which is body language. I realized that since I could not see her eyes, facial expressions, and posture I could not determine if she was being sincere or sarcastic. Although written and telephone communication are tools to aide in our getting acquainted, the best way to get to know someone is face to face communication.

Written Communication

Most professional personnel have Internet access and computers. This allows family and friends to stay acquainted with their loved ones without long distance telephone bills. Electronic communication is instant and an excellent way to stay informed about the current events going on the lives of those we are in relationship with. Internet dating has become popular in our high tech society. Internet dating allows you to view a photograph of an interesting person as well as study their profile before you begin corresponding with them on line. You may get acquainted with them on line as long as you like until you feel comfortable enough to meet the individual in person. Those who decide to get acquainted on line must realize that typing words on a keyboard and relating to someone face to face are as different as night and day.

Some people are led to correspond with those who are incarcerated by letters. This form of outreach is an excellent way to witness Christ to those who are in prison. Not only does the individual who is incarcerated receive exhortation through outside contact but also those who share in this ministry receive an opportunity to serve.

It is not uncommon for a child to write a letter to their non-custodial parent in order to stay in touch between visitations. Sometimes when there is a romantic interest people express their written thoughts through poetry. Letters written to people we have a personal interest is often more expressive than what we would discuss over the telephone or in person. This is because creative people can meditate on what they want to say and communicate their feelings with great passion. One of the best ways to get acquainted with a creative person is to read what they write because they generally write from their heart. Although the different forms of written communication can be good ways to get or maintain an acquaintance they also lack the personal touch of face to face contact.

Telephone Communication

Where would the average teenager be without a telephone? Most would be frustrated at the inability to communicate with their friends. Not only have teenagers become reliant on the telephone most adults are also. Whether we use the contemporary cell phone or the more traditional land-line the telephone has become one of our primary ways to stay connected with one another. We use the telephone to stay in touch with those we have family, ministry, professional, and personal relationships with.

Some people prefer written communication because they feel uncomfortable with the spontaneous conversation that takes place in telephone conversations. Conversely, some people do not like to write but they can talk on the telephone for hours at a time. The telephone is an excellent tool for strangers to get acquainted. Whether the call is local or long distance as long as the other party has a telephone they can talk as long as they have the time.

Parents should monitor the time their minor children stay on the telephone because it could become a distraction from their homework and household chores. It would be appropriate for a parent to establish a schedule for their children with daily times when the telephone is available for personal use. Even adults need to use self-discipline in their telephone use. If we are getting acquainted with a stranger it is possible to spend so much time on the telephone that you feel like you know the person better than you do. If you speak with this person every day for two to three hours at a time it may cause you to move faster through the stages of relationships than you would if you limited your conversation to an hour three or four times a week. If you are married and you are getting acquainted with someone through telephone conversation you need to be careful that you do not neglect your spouse.

In family, ministry, and professional relationships telephone conversations are often used to exchange information more so than get acquainted. When a couple is happily married there is no doubt that the telephone can be used to sustain their acquaintance with one another but there is nothing like being in the company of the one you love. Although telephone conversations are an excellent way to get acquainted in our personal relationships there is no better way to get acquainted than face-to-face communication.

Face to Face Communication

Have you ever spent time with someone who insisted on talking on their cell phone while you pretended not to ease drop? Most sensitive people consider this practice to be rude especially if the objective is spending personal time together. Regardless as to whether the relationship type is family, ministry, professional, or personal, face to face communication where you can give the other person your undivided attention is likely to be a positive foundation for your relationship to grow.

Although written and telephone communication have their place, there are things you learn in a person's presence that you will not learn if they are behind a pen and paper, a computer or a telephone. Face to face communication can aide in getting acquainted in any setting. Going to the grocery store can reveal volumes about a person's character. Why does a person leave their shopping cart in the middle of the aisle when they see someone behind them trying to get by? Perhaps this person is inconsiderate. After taking groceries to the car, does the person return the grocery cart to its designated place or just leave it to cause minor body damage to the next occupant's vehicle? If so, that might be an indication of a thoughtful and considerate person. When dining at a restaurant is the person polite to you but rude to the waitress? This may indicate that there is a difference between the person's personality and character.

Perhaps a person is clumsily tripping while walking down stairs or dribbling water while attempting to look at you and drink at the same time. They may simply be a "goofuss" or nervous in your company. If their smile is forced without any teeth showing and they won't make eye-to-eye contact that may be an indication that although you enjoyed talking with one another on the telephone you may have a negative connection in person. Conversely, if the individual mirrors your body language by maintaining eye to eye contact with a warm smile, that may be an indication of a positive connection.

Whether you decide to allow the relationship to go to the intimate acquaintance stage will depend not just on what you believe God's purpose is for the relationship but also how well you connect in your face to face communication.

Intimate Acquaintance

An intimate acquaintance is a person you consider your self to be close to. This is a person that you feel you can be emotionally vulnerable with. This also may be a person that you socialize with on a regular basis. In 1 Samuel 19:2 we are told that Jonathan warned David of his father's intent to kill him. Jonathan also gave David advice on how to avoid his father's treachery as well as a place to hide. David and Jonathan's relationship has transcended the stranger and casual acquaintance stage in that they have shared the intimate details of one another's lives and they have both demonstrated that they have each others best interest at heart. The Bible says in Proverbs 4:23:

Keep your heart with all diligence for out of it spring the issues of life.

God desires that we protect our heart because that is where the essence of our character is. In family relationships there are those family members we are close to and others we are not. Under most circumstances ministry and professional relationships require varying degrees of intimacy depending on what they believe the purpose of the relationship is.

At my police precinct, the supervisors have an office we all use in common. One of the officers assigned to my precinct was having challenges with his work efficiency and productivity. He made several mistakes that were violations of police department rules and regulations. I had heard so much in the office concerning the officer that I found myself developing a negative image of him although he was a stranger to me. The officer was later assigned to my team and I became his supervisor. Although our interaction initially started out simply as a professional supervisor-subordinate relationship as time went on we moved from being casually acquainted to intimate acquaintances. Our relationship shifted when I discovered he knew Christ and that we connected in other areas of our lives. When he became vulnerable by becoming emotionally transparent, I discovered the reason for his difficulty at work was that he was going through a divorce. Since I have been divorced, I was in a position to encourage him during his season of despair. I learned from that experience that the reported reputation of others is sometimes incomplete because our opinions do not have the sufficient facts needed to draw conclusions that are based on the truth. I also learned that there are some things that you can best learn in the intimate acquaintance stage of a relationship.

The tools that we need to help us navigate through the intimate acquaintance stage are perception, intuition, and discernment.

Perception

Have you ever seen somebody so attractive that you forgot your favorite scripture? If we were honest most of us would answer yes to that question. Perception is the knowledge we acquire through the five senses: sight, hearing, smell, taste, and touch. Sometimes when we see what we believe is physically attractive we allow looks to be the determining factor in our desire to get acquainted. This may be true even for those who are already married. Time has the potential to make our spouses unattractive and we may find ourselves sharing intimate details of our life because we like being in the company of an attractive person. If you listen to the person's positive comments that can be an additionally motivating factor with what you see. If the person smells good wearing your favorite cologne and you're in their presence on a regular basis that can be "the straw that broke the camels back." In the intimate acquaintance stage you begin sharing personal details of your life. There is a potential for a soul-tie to develop at this stage especially if both parties are emotionally vulnerable in the same area. The decision to move into an intimate acquaintance should not be solely based on our perception. What we perceive is subject to our fluctuating emotions therefore our perception is not totally reliable.

Our perception can be reliable when we use it to determine the mood of a person we have an intimate acquaintance with. If you see a frown on their face you may choose to smile or try to encourage them. If you hear a sarcastic tone in their conversation you should inquire as to what the problem is and see if you can offer a solution. Our perception can be a tool that we use to aide us in better understanding those we are in relationship with.

Intuition

Is it true that only women have intuition? The answer is no. Intuition is considered by some to be the sixth sense. It is when we have subliminal knowledge about something without thinking about it. Intuition in humans is like instinct to an animal. If a shark sees a fish thrashing in the water it will instinctively swim toward the fish and when it gets close the shark will open its mouth, shut its eyes, and attempt to devour its prey. These actions are instinctive which means they were not thought out ahead of time. Likewise a good mother intuitively knows that her baby crying is not because the child is hungry but because the child is sick. Her intuition is important because it enables her to respond quickly to the need of her baby. Men have intuition also but often they spend more time developing their perceptive skills than their intuitive skills.

Intuition can best be described as a gut feeling that something is either right or wrong. Intuition is also described as a hunch that you cannot logically explain. Sometimes our intuition is connected to our subliminal memory. If we have had a positive or negative experience in our past and we find ourselves in a similar situation, we may intuitively respond to that situation the way we did in the past without thinking. Intuition is totally subjective, by this I mean that your intuition is a sense that can only be measured by you. Intuition is different from perception in that if two people look at someone wearing a blue suit they both see the blue suit, but those same two people can intuitively sense different things about the same individual. A pure heart is important in the sense of intuition. If you have unforgiveness in your heart your intuition may give you the sense that you should not entertain an intimate acquaintance with someone not because they are in error but because you are in error. Conversely, if you are healed from those negative emotions your intuition may give you peace about going to the next level in your relationship.

The French phrase "je ne sais quoi" in essence means, "I don't know." The phrase is used to describe an intangible positive quality that we intuitively sense in people. This quality is especially noticeable in attractive members of the opposite sex. Sometimes our attraction transcends the long hair, pretty eyes, and athletic build that we perceive is that "special" quality we sense with our intuition. In the event a person is married and they intuitively sense this positive quality in an attractive member of the opposite sex, it would not be advisable to move from a casual to an intimate acquaintance because the personal sharing could possibly lead to an adulterous relationship.

Our perception and intuition are very important tools in determining whether we should move from one stage of relationship to another. However, our most important tool is discernment.

Discernment

How reliable is your perception and intuition? The answer to that question is going to depend on how you interpret your perception and intuition. Both are subjective and dependent on our perspective of what we are experiencing. Discernment is objective. It is not based on our assessment of a matter but on God's judgment. In discernment, the Holy Spirit gives you a conviction that something is right or wrong and that conviction can be supported by a biblical principle. The primary difference between discernment, perception, and intuition is that discernment is a supernatural ability while perception and intuition are natural abilities.

Both discernment and intuition can be confused because they are experienced within. Unfortunately, sometimes you are unable to distinguish the difference until after you have made a decision. If you sense that you should not move from being a casual to an intimate acquaintance and that sense is just a gut feeling that is probably your intuition. However, if you have the same sense and later discover that the person is a liar and cannot be trusted that is discernment because the reason for your decision was not a subjective gut feeling but an objective decision made based on a biblical principle.

Discerning the Right Timing

In baseball, what is the difference between a strike and a homerun? Baseball is a game that is played with a ball and a bat. There are two teams of nine players that alternate playing offense (the team at bat) and defense (the team on the field). The objective of the game is for the batter to hit the ball out of the park (homerun) or somewhere in the field where the defenders cannot get to it before the batter or one of their teammates runs to one of four bases. The fourth base is home. Every time the opposing team crosses home base they score one point. The pitcher throws the baseball over home plate where the batter's objective is to swing at the pitch and hit the ball so that he can score a base hit. If the batter swings at the pitch and misses it is called a strike. The difference between a strike and a homerun is not just the power with which the batter swings the bat but the timing of the swing. If the batter can track the ball with his eyes as it approaches him and swing at the right time with just enough power he can hit the ball out of the park and score a homerun.

Discernment is important in understanding God's timing. When we move from a ministry to a personal relationship or from a casual to intimate acquaintance, success is often determined by timing. Just like baseball when the batter decides it's the right time it might be too soon or too late. Having known the person for less than a month may be a factor to consider in determining if the timing is too soon to go from the simplicity of a casual acquaintance to the vulnerability of an intimate acquaintance. The fact that the person has been recently divorced may be an indication that the timing is not right to move from a ministry relationship to a personal relationship.

It is important to understand that success or failure in relationships is like the thrill of victory or the disdain from defeat in baseball, it is often a matter of timing. You may discern God's timing by being sensitive to the conviction of the Holy Spirit. If you feel uncomfortable about moving forward, it is possible that the Holy Spirit is activating your gift of discernment. Sometimes knowing whether to move forward in your relationship is as simple as discussing the desired change with the person you are in relationship with.

The easiest way to sharpen your discernment is to ask God to give you a greater ability to discern the difference between right and wrong. Not only do you need to pray but you also need to begin studying God's word and apply what you understand to the life situations you face daily. The more you prayerfully apply the word of God to your life on a regular basis the more effective you will become in using your gift of discernment. Whether you are deciding to move from a professional to personal relationship or move from a casual to intimate acquaintance you will need to understand how to use your perception, intuition, and discernment in order to make the right decisions.

Friendship

A friendship transcends the intimate acquaintance stage to a relationship where the individual has proven that they can be a trusted companion. In 1 Samuel 19:4 we are told that when Saul was intent on killing David, Jonathan acted as a friend and spoke on David's behalf. Jonathan's name in the original language means "God's gift." A true friend is a gift from God that He gives not just for the good times but the bad times. Jonathan played a significant role by interceding for David when Saul was a threat to him. There is no doubt that Jonathan was instrumental in saving David's life. This is an indication that a true friend has your best interest at heart even at the expense of his or her own life. The Bible says in Proverbs 17:17:

A friend loves at all times, and a brother is born for adversity.

Friendship is a relationship where love is unconditional between the two people involved. It is not a mere emotional relationship that cannot survive the storms and challenges of life. It is a relationship where your friend will be there for you through thick and thin. Children are born to parents so that the parents can raise a godly offspring. Friends are born to us to be our companions during times of difficulty and adversity. In the intimate acquaintance stage of a relationship you let your guard down and you are transparent about some of the more personal details in your life.

I will never forget the words of my mother when I was a young man. She said, "If you have one true friend in life you have been blessed." I was blessed by God to have a friend during one of the most trying times of my life. My hearts desire has been to keep my ministry relationships separate from my personal relationships because I wanted to protect the integrity of the ministry. Often times, people cannot handle the transition from ministry to personal relationships. Sometimes the people you serve put you on a pedestal because of your position. They often forget that you are flesh and blood and are subject to error just as they are. I am thankful that God gave me grace when I took the chance to become friends with one of my sisters in the ministry. In retrospect, when I look back at that season of my life, I was going through an emotional funk. I was in so much despair I did not care about the ministry and I was ready to give up. My friend stood by me during that difficult season in my life. She prayed for me when I would not pray for myself. She held me when I needed to be held. She listened to me when I needed to vent. She helped me to remember that the most important thing to me has been my relationship with God and the ministry He has called me to. Approximately a year after my dark season, my friend's mother died and I was able to be there in her time of need. Depending on the degree of friendship you engage in, the relationship has the potential to go through the simple, deep, and total disclosure phases.

Disclosure in relationships is a double-edged sword. Sharing intimate details of your life puts you in a position to be betrayed it can also draw you closer to someone.

Simple Disclosure

If you sense that there is a potential friendship brewing between you and another person, the best place to start is by sharing your likes and dislikes. In simple disclosure anything that you share should not have the potential to harm you if the person you share it with chooses not to keep it secret. The purpose for simple disclosure is to establish a connection between you and your potential friend. This is important because it is difficult to establish a friendship with a person that you have nothing in common with. Perhaps both of you were cheerleaders in high school, or maybe both of you served in the same branch of the military. Whatever you have in common has the potential to give you a good idea of the person you are dealing with.

It is important to remember at the simple disclosure stage you are probably dealing with the superficial personality of the individual. This occurs while you are moving from the stranger to casual acquaintance stage of the relationship. Even though simple disclosure is relatively superficial you must be careful not to move too fast too soon. If you are single and lonely or married and frustrated there is a tendency to cling prematurely to people you would like to be friends with. You should always ask God to disclose to you your motive for wanting to be friends. Sometimes we have subconscious needs and desires that we are unaware of. If we cannot be honest with ourselves then we won't be honest with those we desire to build friendships with either. If you cannot honestly say to yourself why you want to be friends with that person, you should not proceed further. If you can, then the parties involved should share their thoughts and feelings about their relationship to see if they are in agreement.

Deep Disclosure

Would you pour water in a cup with holes in it? Some people are like cups with holes in them. If you share the simple details of your life and they are repeated to someone beside your confidant, then that is a signal that you should not share the deep issues of your heart with that individual. When two people find that uniqueness of their connection to one another, there is a natural momentum that has the tendency to lead to deep disclosure. In deep disclosure, you should feel comfortable enough to share intimate details in your life that if repeated could be embarrassing. This is why you need to be prayerful about God's purpose for the relationship. Just because you want a friend does not necessarily mean you can be a friend. Sometimes you will take a risk and move into deep disclosure only to discover that the person you wanted to be friends with desired the privileges of friendship without the responsibility of friendship. Even if you pray without ceasing there are some things that God will not tell you; but He will let you find out because He is allowing you to be tested in order to improve your character. Sometimes you have to pour water in the cup to find out that there are holes in it. It is a privilege to have a friend who will talk to you at 1 a.m. for two hours knowing that he or she has to get up at 6 a.m. for work. It is a privilege to have a friend who will loan you money without demanding an immediate reimbursement when you have an unexpected necessary car repair. It is a responsibility to reciprocate for your friend when they need to talk to you at an inconvenient hour or when they need financial assistance for some emergency purpose. It is through deep disclosure that you discover what people can and cannot handle.

Deep disclosure is not only intended to reveal the weakness of your friend's character but your response to their weaknesses. Sometimes relationships are like a hammer and nails to a building. The hammering is not intended to destroy but to build. If you cannot handle the construction process, you will not be able to handle the friendship. If violence, drug, or alcohol abuse is disclosed you need to know what you can and cannot handle. Sometimes people don't need a friend they may need a counselor or some type of professional help. How close you choose to remain during the season of adversity is going to depend on the depth of your spiritual, emotional, and mental ability. If you cannot handle the issues of your friend, you should pray for their deliverance and if God gives you the peace to stay in the background you can be there for them when they come through.

Total Disclosure

Could you imagine what it would be like to be able to talk to your friend about anything? Who can you tell that you're having homosexual feelings? Who can you tell that you are seriously considering suicide? To be totally honest with God is to be totally honest with you. If a person is not honest with God and themselves, they will not be honest with you. The worst person to deceive is you because not being honest with yourself is living a lie. I could not imagine what it would be like to have to wear make up morning, noon, and night. At some point in time all of us should desire to take off the mask (our make up) and be ourselves with a friend that we know will love us unconditionally.

Total disclosure is complete honesty with your friend. If you have one person in your life that you can tell your deepest, darkest secrets to you are truly blessed. Total disclosure does not mean that you can say or do whatever you want to your friend at the expense of their feelings. Total disclosure is the ability to be completely honest about yourself keeping in mind that you still have to have your friend's best interest at heart.

The truth of the matter is that most friendships have varying degrees of deep disclosure. It is rare to find a total disclosure in the best of friendships but we must never forget that with God all things are possible.

Summary

Although David was a stranger to the nation of Israel before he was anointed king, he did not remain a stranger very long. David was convicted by the Holy Spirit that he needed to do battle against the Philistine giant, Goliath, and when he was victorious the nation became acquainted with him. His fame led to his acquaintance with Jonathan while he served in the court of Saul. Jonathan and David shared their military service in common, which was probably the basis of their casual acquaintance. After becoming intimately acquainted through sharing their more personal issues in common they became friends. Their friendship was tested during Saul's attempts to kill David. Jonathan proved that he was a gift from God when he stood in the gap by obstructing Saul's attempts to kill David.

Jonathan and David's relationship is an excellent biblical illustration of how we can successfully move through the stages of relationships. Whether we are considering a same sex or opposite sex relationship the principles in getting acquainted are fundamentally the same. Once we decide we are going to have a personal relationship with someone the natural tendency is to identify that person as a friend. Calling somebody a friend without going through the stages of relationships is like calling a child an adult simply because they have the body and the outward appearance of an adult yet they have not gone through the developmental process of becoming an adult. When a marriage is in crisis, the tendency is to gravitate toward a relationship that provides comfort. This is a risk and could be perilous to the marriage if the relationship is not allowed to develop over a period of time. When a single person is lonely, finding someone that they connect with has a tendency to incline the people involved in the relationship to move at 100 mph in order to bring comfort to their loneliness. Relationships need time to develop just like an embryo develops from a fetus to a healthy child.

We risk failure in our personal relationships not only if our desire for them does not line up with God and our divine purpose but we are also prone to failure when we move too fast too soon through the stages of relationships. There is no exact equation or formula to determine exactly how long we should remain in each stage of the relationship process; therefore the people involved should make their vertical focus on God primary before their horizontal focus on one another. Communication between the people involved is essential as they move through the stages of relationships. As long as we share a common sense of purpose and we are on one accord, there is hope that we can have successful and rewarding relationships.

CHAPTER FOUR

Biblical Friendship

⁓⧖⁓

(What friendship really is)

If your shadow were to say to you, "I am your friend because I follow you wherever you go," what would you say? Perhaps you would respond by asking "where were you when the sun went down?" When the sun casts its light on the front of an object the opposite side of the object will cast a shadow. The shadow is the image of the part of the object that is not illuminated. When the sun goes down there is no light, when there is no light there will be no shadow. God established a rotation in that every rising and setting of the sun would mark the beginning and ending of each day. Life has the same rotation with light representing good times and darkness representing bad times.

So often we think people are our friends only to discover that when we were in the light of our good times they were with us covering our back just like a shadow. Unfortunately when the darkness of our bad times surfaced they have disappeared just like a shadow. We know that God is with us by His Spirit and that He is our light. He has promised that

He will never leave nor forsake us; therefore He is our best friend. But God is invisible and one of the ways He manifests His love for us is by giving us friends who will be with us in the good times as well as the bad times.

God takes friendship so seriously that out of all the great men in the Old Testament He only referred to two of them as His friends. The two men were Abraham and Moses. In the New Testament out of all the people that had contact with Jesus, He only referred to His disciples as His friends. If God takes friendship seriously, so should we. If God's friends are few and far between, so should ours. One of the highest compliments that you can say to someone is that "I am your friend." Therefore, we should not use that term lightly nor should we make a commitment to friendship without being confident that God has ordained that relationship. In this chapter, we will look at the friendship between Jonathan and David, which is one of the greatest friendships in the Bible. We risk disappointment and heartache when we identify people as friends who have not demonstrated the components of friendship, covenant, love, giving, and trust.

Covenant

A covenant is a promise or a mutual agreement between two or more parties that is binding. In 1 Samuel 18:2, we are told that after Saul's attempt to kill David, Jonathan made a covenant with David because he loved him as himself. Here we see that the friendship between Jonathan and David is affirmed in the midst of adversity. In Psalms 89:3, we are told that God says:

> *I have made my covenant with my chosen David. He has sworn to his servant. David your seed I will establish forever.*

God in His sovereignty selected David with whom to

have a perpetual agreement. In this agreement God promises that one of David's descendants would remain on the throne of Israel forever. This was a Messianic prophesy of Jesus Christ who was to come. Jesus would later be born into the lineage of David and He consequentially becomes the King of Kings.

The promise that God made to establish David's seed on the throne perpetually is called a covenant. In Old Testament times, the covenant of two people's word was like a written contract in contemporary times. From a biblical perspective, the primary difference between a covenant and a contract is that God maintains a covenant while a contract is enforced by the legal system that has jurisdiction where the contract originated. In other words, a covenant is spiritual while a contract is secular. Christians should only enter into covenant with other Christians because the ultimate authority in their agreement is God. Non-Christians are not submitted to God therefore they would not be spiritually bound to keep the covenant. Non-Christians are, however bound to keep a contractual agreement as a matter of law. The principle of covenant not only applies to friendships but to other relationships as well.

Marriage is the primary relationship in which a covenant and contract exist for Christians. When Christians marry, they enter into a covenant at the wedding ceremony to be faithful to one another until death. God witnesses this covenant along with the family and friends who are in attendance. Before the couple gets married they apply for a marriage license, which is signed by the officiating minister on the day of the wedding. The marriage license represents a written contract that legally binds the couple together. I believe that one of the reasons that marriages fail is because the people involved were not true friends in the biblical sense. Covenant is one of the most important parts of a friendship because the agreement to keep covenant binds the friends together when they disagree in other areas. If you cannot keep a covenant of friendship, it will be difficult to keep a covenant of marriage. Covenant friendship should precede marriage just as a musician precedes a performance by rehearsing or an athlete precedes an event by practicing. The more we practice covenant the better we will be at keeping covenant.

My primary ministry relationship has been with the senior pastor of my church for the past fifteen years. Our church is like a family with our pastor serving as our spiritual father. As can be expected in most families, there exists contention between parents and their children. Like many children there were many occasions when I felt like running away from home because like a spoiled child I could not get my way. No matter how frustrated I was I felt like I was on a leash and I could not get a release. After seeking God in the matter, He revealed to me that my spiritual father and I were in covenant with one another and that I did not have the authority to terminate our relationship because God was using it to build character in me. It also occurred to me that I was learning faithfulness by remaining in a difficult situation. The faithfulness that I have learned in my covenant relationship with my spiritual father has helped me to remain faithful in my covenant friendships.

The core of the covenant principle is also contained in the ideas behind the spiritual and the simple vow.

The Spiritual Vow

Have you ever promised God you were going to do something? If the answer is yes, you made a spiritual vow. A spiritual vow is a promise made directly to God in prayer to do something specific. If you promise God you are going to give a specific offering or fast for a specific period of time, you have made a spiritual vow.

A spiritual vow is relevant in a covenant friendship when you promise God directly that you will do something specific in your friendship. If you promise God you will pray for your friend at a specific time each day, you have entered into a spiritual vow as it relates to your covenant friendship.

The Simple Vow

Have you ever loaned somebody some money and they had amnesia when it came time to pay you back? If a person promises to repay a loan at a specific time and they fail to do so, they have broken their simple vow. A simple vow is a promise made to you or to another person. If you promise yourself you are going to go on a diet, you have made a simple vow.

A simple vow is relevant in a covenant friendship when you promise your friend you will do something specific. If you promise your friend you will assist them in their upcoming move or if you promise them you will be at a specific place at a specific time, you have made a simple vow. In our covenant friendships we should make every effort to keep our word.

Love

Love is the nature of God that is expressed when we demonstrate His attitude toward one another in everything that we do. In 1 Samuel 18:3, we are told that Jonathan loved David and that love was demonstrated by his actions. Both Jonathan and David demonstrated a love for one another that transcended mere brotherly affection but was an unconditional sacrificial love that would endure even when they were apart from one another. In 1 John 4:7, it reads:

> *Beloved let us love one another for love is of God and everyone who loves is born of God and knows God. He who does not love does not know God for God is love.*

One of the ways that a Christian demonstrates their love for God is by their love for others. When a person accepts Jesus Christ as their Lord and Savior, the Holy Spirit comes to live inside the believer. The Holy Spirit will lead us to people, places, and things that will challenge us to die to ourselves and demonstrate the unconditional love of God.

When I think of the unconditional love that Jonathan had for David, I am reminded of the friend I mentioned earlier. Not only did she hang in there with me during my emotional funk but she demonstrated love at a time when I was bound by fear. She witnessed my failure to take advantage of several opportunities that may have changed my life for the better. Although she was very frustrated and disappointed with me because of my stubbornness, after the smoke cleared, she always returned to a place of unconditional love. I have learned to use that experience as a positive reference for my sharing love in my future friendships. An a la cart menu is a list of dishes where you pay for each item separately, as opposed to a regular menu where you pay for the entire dish as a whole. Sometimes people want a la cart relationships. By that I mean they are not true friends because they want to pick and choose what they want to love in us and what they do not. I was blessed because my friend loved the good and bad parts of me and I am grateful that God gave her to me as a friend.

Love is translated in the Bible to have different meanings depending on the context in which you find the word. The Old Testament was written in Hebrew and the word love translated means "friendly affection". The New Testament was written in Greek. The Greek language has three primary words to that are used to describe love. These words are agape, phileo, and eros. These specific words are not found in the biblical account of Jonathan and David but the principles they represent are relevant to all relationships, especially friendships.

Agape

Do you remember your first love? How do you feel about them now? It is possible that you no longer have the same level of emotional feeling toward that person. This may be because your feelings were not rooted in God's unconditional love. Agape is not a feeling it is the very nature and character of God because "God is love." While we were trapped in our sin, God sacrificially gave His Son, Jesus, to die for us. God's motivation for this ultimate act of kindness was love. We call it unconditional because it was done without the expectation of receiving anything in return. Unconditional love will have you be patient with a person even when the person is not worthy of your patience. Can you honestly say you had this type of love for your first love? Some people have become enemies with the person that they have loved so dearly. However when we practice unconditional love we may find that God has made our enemies our footstool and given us too much love to step on them. This is especially true when we do not focus on what we have gone through with that person but where we are going with them. By this I mean that friendship is not only a relationship but it is a destination that is motivated by love.

When God commands that we love one another, He is saying we should have His attitude in our relationships with one another. If you are kind when your friend is rude to you and the motivation for the kindness is that you wanted to be more like God, you have demonstrated love. If you are forgiving when your friend did not keep their promise to pick you up when your car broke down, you have demonstrated love as long as the focus of your action was God.

Although God commands us to love everyone, this attitude is especially relevant in our friendships. It is inevitable that our friends will disappoint us in some way, shape, or form because we all are human and subject to make mistakes. If a person is your friend, you are not only obligated to be patient with them in their failure because of the covenant that exist between you but you are also obligated to be faithful to them because you love them with the love of the Lord.

This love does not require you to be foolish, if your friend gets caught in some immoral, illegal, or unethical activity. The Holy Spirit may lead you to give them some space or maybe even seek an objective third party who can help your friend deal with their issue. Tough love does not interfere when it is obvious that the adversity that your friend is facing is God's way of testing and building their character. As a friend you will be able to determine your level of involvement by praying and asking God to show you the way. If you can keep the confidence of your friend, perhaps you may need to go outside the relationship to get counseling on how you can be of assistance. If you believe you are led by the Holy Spirit to go outside the relationship, you want to be confident that the person you are confiding in can be trusted not to violate the confidence of you and your friend.

Phileo

Do you think you will always like your friend? The answer to that question is obviously "no." This is the reason that our friendships have to transcend the vacillating emotions of "I like you" one day and "I don't like you" the next day. Although agape is the most important type of love in our friendships, a friendship without phileo will be empty and shallow. Phileo can be defined as tender affection. While agape is considered to be unconditional love, phileo is brotherly love. Phileo is different from agape because it is rooted in your feelings and emotions for one another as opposed to agape, which is rooted in your attitude and the choice to love unconditionally.

One of the hindrances to the emotions we have in phileo is when our friend either disappoints us or commits an offense against us. If your friend gets delivered from smoking cigarettes and later suffers a relapse that could possibly affect your feelings about the friendship. The anger that you might feel when you see them smoking like a chimney might be greater than the joy you felt when they got delivered. Your friendship might take another hit if when you try to offer your help they tell you to "mind your own business". Under these circumstances your feelings about the friendship may be in jeopardy. Therefore, your response to your friend should be the patience that is motivated by agape love. Prayerfully, the phileo love will be restored over a period of time after you have forgiven your friend for offending you.

Would you like your creditors to waive the outstanding balance on any bills you might owe? If the answer is yes then you understand the essence of the principle of forgiveness. Forgiveness is the act of emotionally releasing a person from the penalty of the offense committed against you. Forgiveness and forgetting, however are not the same. In forgiveness, you may have a memory of what offended you but you are no longer disturbed by it because you have let it go. In forgetting, you do not have any memory about a specific incident. There is nothing wrong with remembering what your friend did to offend you, but when you throw it up in their face or constantly remind them of the offense that is evidence that you have not forgiven them. Additionally, if you are repeatedly requiring your friend to pay for the offense committed against you, perhaps you should ask God to give you the ability to forgive them. One of the ways you know that you have forgiven them is that the tenderness and affection of phileo love will return. It is important for us to practice forgiveness not just to restore the affection in our friendships but we must also understand that if we do not forgive others God will not forgive us. We must be mindful that one day the shoe may be on the other foot and we may need our friend to forgive us so that we may enjoy the fullness of phileo love with one another.

Eros

Have you ever had a member of the opposite sex express their attraction to you and you said, "Let's just be friends." Most of the time when a person says, "we are just friends" to a member of the opposite sex they are not speaking of biblical friendship. What they are really saying is, "I am not attracted to you." Eros can best be described as the feelings that are stimulated by sexual desire. Erotic love is stimulated when members of the opposite sex are attracted to one another. Erotic love begins as a sensual feeling and is sometimes expressed by engaging in sexual activity.

It is relatively easy for some men and women to be friends as long as erotic love is not present. But when men and women share things in common and decide to become friends, they need to be honest about their feelings. Sometimes a man or woman will say they are friends just to get close to someone they are attracted to. It is possible they may not understand that they are experiencing erotic love and those desires are motivating them instead of agape's unconditional love. We must ask ourselves if we were not attracted to the person would we still want to be their friend. If the answer is no, we should retreat and re-evaluate the reason for wanting to be their friend. If the answer is yes, we should have enough courage to discuss our feelings with our friend. It is dishonest to call a person your friend and know you have erotic feelings and not tell them. If you are afraid to be honest with the person for fear it will jeopardize your friendship, then I question the character and strength of your friendship. Both people in the friendship need to be aware of one another's feelings so that the relationship can be built on the truth and not a lie. If we find ourselves in this situation, we need to pray and ask for God's guidance and try to maintain an open line of communication with one another.

Sometimes married people develop friendships with members of the opposite sex. This should not be a problem as long as both spouses are in agreement and the friendship does not take precedence over the marriage. But when erotic love develops between friends, if one or both of the people are married, wisdom says the relationship either needs to be modified or suspended. A modification of the relationship could include spending less personal time together or speaking with one another less frequently. Suspensions are generally more painful yet necessary. One might involve discontinuing contact or communication with the possibility of reconciling the friendship if the erotic feelings subside. It is important to understand that the marriage covenant should always take precedence over the friendship covenant.

The mere presence of erotic love does not have to lead to sexual immorality any more than the mere presence of agape love leading to friendship. Erotic love is a sensual feeling like phileo love is an emotional feeling. When we experience these feelings, we choose to act on them or not to act on them. The choice not to act on erotic feelings is a product of self-discipline. It is possible for men and women to be friends with agape, phileo, and erotic love as long as there remains an open and honest line of communication. When a single man and woman have a reciprocal erotic desire for one another and their friendship has been proven and tested, perhaps they should prayerfully consider marriage as a way to take their friendship to the next level.

Giving

Giving is when we share our possessions with others. In 1 Samuel 18:3, we are told that Jonathan's love for David was not just demonstrated through words but by what he was willing to sacrificially give David. Jonathan's love manifested itself when he gave his robe, which symbolized his authority as prince to David. It demonstrated that Jonathan knew David would eventually become king. Jonathan not only gave a symbol of his royal authority but he also gave symbols of his military authority. David, in turn, did not have any tangible material to give Jonathan, but he gave his loyalty and support, which are qualities that cannot be measured by dollars and cents. In John 3:16, we read:

> *For God so loved the world that He gave His*
> *only begotten son.*

God's love for us expressed itself in His giving us the greatest gift that can be given to anyone and that is the gift of giving one's self. When God gave us His Son, Jesus, to die for our sins, He gave Himself because God is the Father, the Son, and the Holy Spirit. God did not stop giving with His Son but He followed up by giving us the Holy Spirit who comes to live inside of us upon our confession of faith in Christ. God continues in His generosity by giving us friends to be with us in our times of adversity. God has proven to us that He is our friend because He cares enough to give us the best.

Before I got promoted to police supervisor, I served as a field-training officer who provided on-the-job training for officers who recently graduated from the police academy. I became very close with one of the officers that I trained with when I discovered we shared the same faith. We not only shared a spirit-to-spirit connection through Christ but we also shared a soul-to-soul connection because we had similar life experiences that caused us to bond together. We became friends and stayed in touch after his training was complete. Many years later I got shot in the leg while looking for a domestic violence perpetrator. While I was at home recovering from my injury, my friend came by and brought me groceries. I did not ask him for any assistance but he gave it anyway. I will always remember his gift and generosity. I was one of the groomsmen in his wedding and we remain friends to this day.

Alms

Have you ever met a stingy person? The answer to that question is probably yes. When a person is stingy, it is often due to misunderstanding the significance of giving. The tithe is one tenth of your gross income that you give to the Lord through your local church. An offering is anything above and beyond the tithe. An area of giving that many are not familiar with is alms. Alms are separate from the tithe and offering because they are those gifts that we give to people who are in need.

There will always be poor people among us that we should give to as we are led by the Holy Spirit. However, we have a special responsibility to give to our family and friends. If it is possible we should set aside money for alms in our personal budget, so when our friend has a financial need we will be able to assist in fulfilling that need.

When giving alms to our friends, we need to be prayerful that we have no hidden agenda for our giving other than our covenant relationship and the unconditional love for God and our friend. This is important is because I have learned that if anything can mess up a friendship money can. Each person needs to be led of the Holy Spirit but you may want to avoid loaning your friend money that you cannot afford to lose. If your friend cannot pay you back in a timely fashion and that money is needed for an important bill, the loan could put your friendship in jeopardy. This is the reason you should already have alms set aside to give in a time of need. Once you have given your alms to your friend there should be no expectation to receive anything in return.

If you do not have alms to give your friend you may have to sacrifice getting that pair of shoes or eating out for the next month so that you can assist in providing for the financial need of your friend. It is imperative that you are open to the guidance from the Holy Spirit to determine your level of assistance.

Reciprocal Giving

Have you ever felt like you were giving more than you received in return? If your answer is yes, have you ever considered the fact that some people do not have what you have to give? Therefore, they cannot give to you reciprocally. Do you give in order to receive something in return or do you give because you are in a covenant relationship that has its foundation in God's unconditional love? If you are feeling resentful because you have given to someone who has not reciprocated, it is possible that you gave with the wrong motive. We should never give reluctantly or under compulsion because a gift can only be truly appreciated when it is given cheerfully. After you have sought God in the matter, it would be a good idea to discuss your feelings with your friend. Although your friendship will be tested by your honesty, it will be good for both people to understand how the other is feeling.

It is important to understand that everybody does not have the same ability to give. A turnip cannot give you milk because there is no milk in a turnip. It makes no sense to become frustrated with someone who does not give you what you give in return because if they had what you gave them then they would not have needed you to give it to them in the first place. A simple note of advice: if you have received money from your friend to pay your movers, you could reciprocate by being thoughtful enough to give your friend a "thank you" card or perhaps if your friend has bought you groceries in a time of need, there is nothing wrong with you reciprocating with a home-cooked meal.

Reciprocal giving far transcends financial giving to any selfless act that has your friend's best interest at heart. Perhaps you could save your friend the cost of childcare by babysitting or maybe you could provide transportation for your friend when their car is in the shop. Perhaps you could make the ultimate sacrifice by watching your friend's pet when they are on vacation, even though you do not like animals! The point is that the evidence that someone is your friend is that they are willing to sacrificially give to you. The evidence that you are a friend is that you are willing to sacrificially give to your friend. With this in mind is your best friend really your *friend*? Or better yet are *you* truly their friend?

Surety

What should you do if you have co-signed on a loan for your friend? If you have become a surety for a person you have given them your name by entering into a contractual arrangement where you agree to pay a debt if the person you have co-signed for defaults on the debt. Although, on the surface this may appear to be an act of giving motivated by unconditional love, biblically, it is not wise. The quintessence of Proverbs 6:1-3 says that if you have become a surety for your friend, you should do everything you can to get released from that arrangement. Your friend may need a co-signer because they have failed to establish credit. If this is the case, perhaps your friend needs to delay any major purchases and obtain a credit card with the minimum credit limit in order to establish credit over time. Your friend may need a co-signer due to a history of bad credit. It is possible that you will make a bad situation worse. In this case, what your friend needs is tough love, self-discipline, and a budget instead of you co-signing for more credit. Perhaps you can assist them by encouraging them to get professional help if you do not have the financial expertise to assist your friend in becoming a better steward of their financial resources. If you have already become a surety for your friend you may also need profes-sional financial counseling to assist yourself in getting released from your surety. As their friend you should assume the responsibility of keeping them accountable if they seek financial counseling.

I realize that we do not live in a perfect world and that your child may need you to co-sign for them on their student loan or your sister may need you to co-sign on her house after a divorce. Regardless as to whether it is a family, ministry, professional, or personal relationship becoming a surety is unwise. An analysis of other financial options should also be conducted; becoming a surety should be a last resort.

Trust

Trust is when you are secure with someone and you have confidence and hope in them. In 1 Samuel 19:2, we are told that Jonathan warned David of his father's intention to kill David. Jonathan also advised David to seek a place of safety. Jonathan proved he was David's friend because he stood up against his own flesh and blood in order to remain faithful to his covenant friendship. This incident not only shows that Jonathan could be trusted to guard David's best interest but it also illustrates that sometimes the spiritual bond of friendship is greater than the natural bond of the family. Not only did David trust Jonathan but Jonathan trusted David to protect his family in his absence. This illustrates how trust should be reciprocal in friendships. Proverbs 3:5-6 reads:

> *Trust in the Lord with all your heart; and lean not to your own understanding. In all your ways acknowledge Him, and He will direct your paths.*

The foundation of our trust should not be in our friends or family or in any other relationship. Our trust should be in God. God is the Creator. If we can trust the Sun to rise in the morning and set in the evening, we *should* trust the One who causes the sun to rise and set. We begin our relationship with God through child-like faith in believing that He gave His only begotten Son to die for our sins. As we grow in faith, He leads us to and through situations that build our trust in Him. When we look back at these situations with spiritual eyes we see that it was God who brought us through those situations. It is God's intention that our trust will grow in Him and we will not trust our own understanding but we will be confident that He has our best interest at heart. We also trust that God will lead us by the Holy Spirit within. Therefore, we trust that God will lead us to those people that He desires we have friendships with. Sometimes God will allow us to follow our own understanding in relationships so that we can see by the outcome that the relationship was not of Him.

As I reflect on the importance of trust, I recall the season just after my divorce. I met an individual at my church and we began our acquaintance because we shared similar ministry concerns. In time, I went from the basic sharing in our casual acquaintance to more personal details in our intimate acquaintance. I later discovered that issues that I shared in confidence with this person were repeated to a third party without my consent. I remember feeling like I was naked and as if someone uncovered me. In retrospect, I realized that I was emotionally vulnerable due to my divorce and that I had entrusted the individual with personal information that would have been better kept to myself. The individual later revealed to me that they desired a friendship, but when I reflected on our relationship it occurred to me that this person had likewise betrayed the confidence of others. By sharing personal details with me about others (which were none of my business) this person demonstrated that they could not be trusted. I was also convicted because I allowed this individual to share with me intimate details of others without redirecting the conversation. I became even more sensitive to the need for trust as I grew in my professional and ministry career. I have witnessed people at work and at church betray one another right and left. My experience has taught me to value the friends I can trust and to take a sober view of those who claim they want to be friends but have not demonstrated that they can be trusted.

Emotional Catharsis

Many of the foods that are in our diets have preservatives that once digested are converted into toxins in our bodies. Catharsis is the medical term used for cleansing the digestive system of these dangerous toxins. Catharsis is also a psychological term used to describe the purging and release of negative repressed thoughts and feelings by discussing those issues. In life it is inevitable that we will have negative experiences that have the potential to become emotionally toxic when they are not processed properly. If we do not purge ourselves of those negative emotions they can deteriorate into anger and bitterness.

The enemy of emotional catharsis is distrust. In order to have a quality friendship we need to believe we have the freedom to talk about our negative emotions without our confidence being violated. Distrust is like termites to the frame of a house. Distrust undermines the frame a friendship stands on because trust is the key support in a good friendship. A good friendship cannot stand without trust because the ability to be vulnerable and transparent with your friend is invaluable. If you have to repress your thoughts and emotions around that person, I question the integrity of your friendship. That does not mean you should say whatever you want to say whenever you want to say it just because that person is your friend. Before you share whatever is bothering you, it is important to consider how your friend will respond. If it were an issue that is specific to your relationship, it would be wise to ask God to give you wisdom in how to say what you have to say as well as providing the appropriate time.

Your friend may be suffering from the ramifications of child abuse or domestic violence. If this is the case, you may not be spiritually, mentally, or emotionally equipped to help them with what is troubling them. If you recognize that you are in over your head, it may not be enough to pray the problem away. Your friend may need biblical or professional psychological counseling. You should encourage them to seek counseling and assist them in any way possible.

Security

Have you ever betrayed the confidence of a friend and your friend found out? It is likely that this betrayal has undermined the security of your relationship. Security is the feeling of safety hope and peace. If your friend does not feel secure around you it may be because of the absence of trust. Perhaps you should discuss with one another the reasons for the feelings of insecurity. It is possible they may be projecting unresolved issues onto you. If that is the case, trust is likely to grow when your friend sees that you remain faithful to the friendship despite adversity.

Wisdom says that there are times when you may need to violate the trust of your friend. If you break a trust it should be for a good reason. What will you do if your friend is committing adultery on their spouse and they want to use you as a cover? What will you do if your friend steals something and wants to hide it in your house? Your friend should not be secure in the fact that they can make you a party to their immoral, illegal, or unethical activity. Perhaps you are thinking, 'no one is perfect.' You are right, but your responsibility as a friend is to confront sin not go along with it. The mere fact that your friend would put you in moral, legal, or ethical jeopardy is an indication that they may be selfishly using you and in truth they cannot be your friend. Your friend needs to be confident that you are secure in doing the right thing. This does not mean being self-righteous or holier-than-thou but it does mean that you protect the integrity of your friendship by trying to do the right thing.

Comfort

Is your best friend a man or a woman? Sometimes members of the same sex are better friends because they share more things in common. If a man is weak sexually, he is likely to confide his character flaw to another man if they have built trust in sharing one another's weaknesses. If a woman overeats, she is more likely to confide her character flaw to another woman who can relate. The common denominator in trust is comfort. Comfort is when you receive relief in a time of tension or trouble. There are times when men and women do not feel comfortable with one another because they do not trust that a member of the opposite sex will respond to their issue with understanding.

Some men and women have had negative experiences with members of the opposite sex. Then, they pack their distrust in a bag and bring it with them to other opposite sex relationships. This creates a barrier between men and women that hinders their ability to be comfortable with one another. Where there is no comfort, there is no trust. Where there is no trust, there is no friendship. Some women have had problems with other women gossiping, which causes them to feel more comfortable around men than other women. Likewise, men have sometimes been betrayed by other men, which cause them to feel more comfortable around women than other men.

If we look at our friendships over the course of our lives and see a pattern, we need to ask God why. Why is it you only feel comfortable in friendships with members of the same sex? Why is it that we only trust friendships with people of our race or culture? Why is it that we only feel like we can trust talking to people in a specific age group? Perhaps you feel uncomfortable and trust people who do not challenge you to grow or keep you accountable. If you want to know if a person is your friend ask yourself the following questions:

- Do both of you sense a connection to one another that you cannot fully explain?
- Do both of you make time to be there for one another when ever possible?
- Do both of you take the time to listen to one another objectively?
- Do both of you offer advice to one another without being judgmental?
- Do both of you feel that each of you can be trusted to keep one another's secrets?
- Do both of you feel comfortable enough around one another to be yourselves without any pretense?
- Do both of you love one another unconditionally?

If the answer to all of the above questions is yes you definitely are friends. If you are uncertain about the answer to any of the above listed questions ask God to expose the heart of the individual you would like to become your friend. God will answer you through what the person say's and does.

Ultimately, we must understand that true friends are given to us by God, which means that they will not always meet our paradigm of what we believe a friend should be. As a matter of fact, sometimes we will not be comfortable with our friends because God is using them to force us out of our comfort zone. Show me your friends and I will show you your future. By this I mean that those who are closest to us are a reflection of who we really are. Most of us have heard the saying: "birds of a feather flock together." If you hang around chickens you will have difficulty flying but if you hang around eagles it is likely that they will inspire you to sore with them. Perhaps you have heard the saying: "don't spend major time with minor people." Everyone has value in God's sight but everyone does not have an individual value to us as friends. If a person is not willing to keep covenant and love you unconditionally they may be considered as a minor person as it relates to your friendship with them. If you do not like your friends it is important that you change before you try to get them to change. It is possible that they will never be all you think they should be but God still desires to use you in their lives. Regardless as to the quality of our friendship our ultimate trust has to be that God is leading us and that He has our best interest at heart.

Summary

Jonathan and David's relationship is one of the best examples of friendship in the Bible. Their relationship illustrates that God does not just give friendships for the good times but He also gives friendships for the bad times. Jonathan was heir to the throne of Israel because he was Saul's first born. Jonathan demonstrated his friendship by entering into a covenant of unconditional love with David despite the fact that their relationship would mean he would not become king. His love was displayed not just through brotherly affection but by the kindness he showed through his dedication for David in his time of need. His love was also displayed by giving gifts that had great monetary value to David. Jonathan proved that he could be trusted when he stood against his father, Saul, on David's behalf. Jonathan was in a better position to demonstrate acts of friendship than David was because he had more to offer due to his position in life. David was able to repay Jonathan by keeping their covenant after Jonathan's death by providing covering and protection for his family.

Most of us have unknowingly risked identifying people as friends only to discover that the relationship was not based on covenant, love, giving and trust. We thought they were friends in the light of our good times only to discover that when the darkness of our bad times come those relationships were exposed for what they truly were. Sometimes we are more focused on having a friend than being a friend. If we expect our friends to be faithful to their covenant commitment of friendship, we must keep our covenant as well. If we expect our friends to love us unconditionally, we need to love them unconditionally also. If we expect our friends to be giving, we should be giving also. If we expect our friends to be trustworthy, we need to prove that we can be trusted. The bottom line is that in our friendships we will reap what we sow.

Friendships should be stable but never stand still. Life sometimes brings unemployment, illness, marriage, and children. These changes will not allow a friendship to stand still. If we remain focused on our covenant commitment to God and our friendships, then our relationships can have stability. Yes, there will be times when God may release us from the responsibility we have to our friends due to relocation, marriage or some other event but we need to be prayerful and discerning about when to move or when to remain in our friendships because we never know when we will need our friend or when they will need us. Our friendships will always be at risk when we do not make God our foundation because He will always be our best friend.

CHAPTER FIVE

Dating, Courtship, and Marriage

❖

(Romance God's style)

Air traffic controllers are tasked with the responsibility of coordinating the safe operations of hundreds of aircraft at any given time. They keep the aircraft at a safe distance from one another, direct them around bad weather, and ensure that air traffic flows with a minimum of delays. What if the pilot and the co-pilot of a commercial airliner could not agree on whether or not they would follow the directions of their air traffic controller? If the pilot is pulling up and the co-pilot is pulling down there is a risk of a crash. In order to have a safe flight the pilot and the co-pilot have to be in agreement that they will follow the direction of the air traffic controllers.

God is our heavenly air traffic controller. He has predetermined our paths from eternity and it is for that reason we should follow His directions. In marriage, the husband should be like the pilot and the wife should be like the co-pilot. If they are not in agreement they risk the possibility of not having a healthy relationship. This is the reason it is essential that the husband and the wife have an individual and collective relationship with God, this way He will be the final authority in their lives. Webster's Collegiate Dictionary defines romance as " a long work of fiction less realistic than a novel." Often times in our western society we approach male female relationships from the unrealistic romantic point of view instead of from the biblical perspective. In this chapter, we will review dating, courtship, and marriage. Additionally we will pay special attention to marriage highlighting the importance of being in a relationship that unifies a man and a woman with spiritual, soulish and physical connection.

Dating

Dating can be defined as the social engagements between men and women who have a potential interest that extends beyond friendship. The essence of Proverbs 22:6 says that fathers have the responsibility for training their children. Dating as practiced in contemporary Western society was non-existent. In Hebrew tradition fathers not only provided for their children's education but they also had the responsibility of circumcising their sons, teaching them a trade and finding them a mate. Apparently David's father, Jesse, abdicated his paternal responsibility when David went to serve as Saul's armorbearer. Initially Saul arranged for David to marry his oldest daughter, Merab, but she was later given to another man. Some time later Saul's youngest daughter, Michal fell in love with David and he subsequently asked for her hand in marriage. Saul told David he would give Michal to David if he brought him 100 foreskins of the Philistines. When David was successful he married Michal.

In our contemporary society it is rare that parents pre-arrange the marriage of their children, this has led to the practice of dating. Dating for Christians can be very difficult because the Bible gives us no explicit instructions on dating relationships. Therefore those who are going to embark upon a dating relationship should pray and ask for God's wisdom on how to proceed. One of the most important questions to ask God is "what is the purpose for this relationship?" This is important because God may reveal to you that the purpose of the relationship is to co-labor together in your ministry or your profession. His will may be that the relationship be professional in nature deplete of personal affection and emotional intimacy. Alternatively, if a man and a woman have sought The Lord about their relationship and they have the peace of God to move forward their next step should include clearly communicating their expectations of one another. Have you ever met somebody who didn't know what they wanted? If the answer is yes this may be due to the individual looking for the right person when they are the wrong person. By this I mean it is more important for the single person to know what God's purpose is in their life than knowing how or when to date. Our relationship choices should not only be based on our understanding our likes and dislikes, our strengths and weaknesses but most importantly our purpose and understanding what season of life we are in. It is possible that one party may simply want companionship due to their just exiting a relationship and the other party may want a relationship that could lead to marriage. In this case we can avoid unnecessary hurt feelings simply by understanding where we are in our walk with God.

Is it true that there is somebody for everybody? I believe that the answer to the question is based on Isaiah 4:1 which says that the day will come when the ratio of women to men will be 7 to 1. It is common knowledge that in most church's single women outnumber single men. If a woman is determined not to compromise God's standard she must be willing to remain single and find contentment in her purpose. In Matthew 19:12 Jesus talks about eunuchs, which was a term that was symbolically given to someone who has the gift of singleness. Those who have the gift of singleness fall into the following 3 categories:

- Those who are born with the gift of singleness.
- Those who through some life experience with another person chose the gift of singleness.
- Those who chose the gift of singleness for the kingdom's sake.

Those who have the gift of singleness choose not to date or pursue marriage. Unfortunately those with the gift of singleness are sometimes made to feel as if they are not normal when nothing is further from the truth. Those who have the gift of singleness are people who can give their undivided attention to God and their purpose.

Those who are interested in dating courtship and marriage may ask, "do I have to date a person that I am attracted to in order to get to know them?" The answer is no. In my opinion the telephone is a marvelous invention. The reason I say this is because you can disqualify people that you have a potential interest in simply by talking to them over the telephone for an extended period of time. Consider this: why spend valuable time and money with someone who you can't hold a decent telephone conversation with? Most people talk about what's really important to them, so if in your telephone conversations you realize that your values are different it would be wise to discontinue considering them as a potential dating partner. If you understand yourself and what you want out of life telephone conversations are a good step in finding out if you want to go to the next level.

Many Christians say, "I don't want to date, I just want to

meet my mate and get married." This is understandable because dating can require a great deal of emotional energy that many people would prefer to save for their mate. God is sovereign and He can order our footsteps to that person. Unfortunately some people will date multiple partners before finding someone they want to spend the rest of their life with. This is why it will require wisdom for us to take our time as we move through the stranger, casual acquaintance, intimate acquaintance and friendship stages of our relationships. While some people want to date to marry others desire to date casually to meet their opposite sex companionship needs. Since there is such a potential for emotional confusion by dating multiple partners I recommend that dating only be used as a process to get to know a person that you consider as a potential spouse. Each individual needs to ask God to show them the thoughts and intents of their hearts so that they can be honest with themselves and those they have relationships with.

Perhaps you are wondering, "Who should initiate the dating relationship, the man or the woman?" Although scripture does not give us clear instructions on how to date, we can use the biblical principle of headship as an example. Biblically the man is head and has responsibility for leadership in the home, therefore he should assume the responsibility for initiating the dating relationship. As a rule, whoever initiates the dating relationship is taking the responsibility of placing themselves in the pilot's seat. In essence when a woman approaches a man in a dating relationship she is assuming the responsibility of headship in the relationship. Although it is common for some women to initiate dating relationships this practice does not line up with biblical principle. Along the same line the question is asked, "Who should pay for the date?" The answer is found in the headship principle, if a man is going to initiate the date he should assume all responsibility for the date unless some other agreement is made before hand. Communication is important in the dating relationship because sometimes one or both parties assume they are entitled to privileges associated with the relationship. Some men assume they are entitled to sex with women especially if they date her on a regular basis. Some women assume that the man they are dating has the financial responsibility of meeting their needs. Sex and financial responsibility are obligations that are unique to marriage and this should be made clear between those who choose to engage in a dating relationship. As a man I look forward to paying for a date with a woman with whom I enjoy her company but I do not want to feel as if I am being used. Therefore if it is practical I suggest those who decide to date one another should share in the financial responsibility of their relationship.

After my divorce I lost interest in dating. One day while cleaning one of the bathrooms in my house I discovered that the water in the toilet had evaporated. I realized that this was due to my only using the bathroom in my bedroom and because I was living alone. At that moment it was as if my singleness slapped me in the face and I realized that I wanted to share my home with someone special. It occurred to me that if I wanted something different I had to do something different. For me this meant that I had to give careful thought to dating. For those single adults like myself who will consider a dating relationship I suggest that you can engage in any social activity that is not immoral, illegal or unethical. These activities could include dinner, theater, movies, concerts and athletic events. These activities should include common interest while exploring other areas of individual interest to help establish a repertoire of knowledge about one another.

As I minister to single adults throughout the nation I have discovered that many are more concerned about the activity they will participate in while on the date than the person they are dating. Sometimes single people are interested in others because of what they can do not because of who they are. Other times dating relationships are pursued as an answer to loneliness and not out of a sincere interest in the other person. Personally I am more interested in the person I date than the activity we share while on a date, which makes the person more important than the activity.

Courtship

Courtship can be defined as an exclusive relationship between a man and a woman that has marriage as its goal. In I Samuel 18:22, David is required to pay a dowry before he marries Michal. In Bible times the man would bring gifts, money or property to the father of the bride to show he was responsible enough to take her as his wife. Likewise, the father of the bride would give a dowry to the husband to help the newly-weds establish their own home. Saul asked for a dowry of 100 foreskins of the Philistines but David in turn provided 200 foreskins of the Philistines. David's presentation of the dowry to Saul demonstrated he was interested in courting and committed to marry Michal.

Courtship is different from dating in that courtship the level of commitment is more serious. For many people dating is like shopping, you try on different items until you find what suits you. Conversely, courtship is when you have found what you are looking for and you are ready to make the purchase. When two people are dating they may or may not consider their partner as a potential spouse and the relationship is on trial; but in a courtship the relationship has passed the test and marriage becomes the objective of the relationship. In Bible times couples did not date for a season, then court for a season, later get engaged then marry. The courtship and engagement were integrated into what was called betrothal. In courtship the couple's intention to marry may or may not be public knowledge, but in betrothal there is a public pledge to marry.

Should couples participate in a pre-marital counseling before they get married? The answer is yes. I am one of the pre-marital counselors at my local church and I have found that once you detail the biblical responsibilities of marriage and highlight areas where the couple may not be compatible they sometimes reconsider their plans to marry. Sometimes couples commit to marriage without going through the process of simple and deep disclosure. If the couple has not discussed their credit report, medical, and employment history I believe they do not know enough about one another to marry. This lack of transparency is a clear indication of a lack of trust, which is the foundation of a true friendship. It is likely that the couple will marry without being friends and having an open and honest relationship. This would be like building a house on a cracked foundation. Extensive pre-marital counseling is designed to expose the cracks in the foundation of the relationship and give the couple the option of making the necessary corrections or abandoning their plans for marriage altogether. If the couple is not at a church that provides extensive pre-marital counseling it would be a worthwhile investment to seek professional Christian counseling outside the church before they get married. If we can spend thousands of dollars on a wedding, surely we can spend a few hundred on pre-marital counseling.

Marriage

Marriage can be defined as the lifelong covenant union between a man and a woman that is not only binding by law but by their love for one another and Christ. In I Samuel 18:27 we see that David married Saul's daughter, Michal. It is very likely that David's relationship with Michal had a spiritual, soulish, and physical connection. In I Thessalonians 5:23 the Bible says:

Now may the God of peace Himself sanctify you completely and may your whole spirit, soul and body be preserved blameless at the coming of our Lord Jesus Christ.

God is a triune being. This unique characteristic of God is sometimes hard to understand. To be triune simply means to consist of three parts or forms. In the same way that water can be seen in three forms; liquid, solid, and gas, God, who created the water, makes Himself known in three forms. He is God the Father, the Creator and Sovereign Ruler of the universe. He is Jesus Christ, the Living Word, who became flesh and dwelt among us. He is the Holy Spirit, the One, who resides inside our human spirit when we accept Jesus Christ, as our Savior. In Genesis 1:26, we see that God created man in His image to be a triune being like Himself. Man is composed of three parts: spirit, soul, and body. Our spirit is the part of our human make-up that receives from God and communicates with God. Our soul is the part of our human make-up where our thoughts and feelings reside. Our body is the part of our human make-up that houses our spirit and soul. Any marriage that does not build the spiritual, soul-ish, and physical connections will not be balanced and bears risk of failure. When I was married, I did not have the wisdom to maintain the three-fold connection with my wife. We did not share in the same sense of spiritual connection to purpose, which affected my desire to pray for the success of our relationship. Our soulish connection was hindered not only by the absence of a spiritual connection but by my lack of understanding on how to love my wife unconditionally. Since there was no balance spiritually and soulishly the physical part of my relationship suffered. The failure of my marriage has taught me a positive lesson about the significance importance of balance in a healthy marriage.

The Spiritual Connection

The spiritual connection in marriage occurs when the man and woman pursue having an individual and collective relationship with God for the purpose of deepening their marital bond. This is more than the salvation that comes from the confession of faith in Christ but walking with God long enough to be able to discern His voice and to make decisions based on biblical principles.

Many of the Psalms were written by David and they illustrate his intimate spiritual connection with God. I can only imagine how much of his relationship with God poured over into his relationship with Michal. Not only was David spiritually connected to his wife, Michal but he was also spiritually connected to his friend Jonathan. Unfortunately, there are those who project their homosexual agenda onto the loving relationship between Jonathan and David, some would even like to use their relationship as biblical support for domestic partnerships. It is important to note that Jonathan and David were friends not sexual partners. At this season of David's life his sexual desires were met through his wife, Michal. We will see that God intended that the spiritual connection of marriage is intended for a man and a woman. The Bible says in Genesis 1:27:

> *So God created man in His image; in the image of God He created Him; male and female He created them.*

Not only are we created in the image of God but amongst living beings He has created two different sexes in that we are all either male or female. Regardless as to whether you are male or female, we have the same fundamental nature in God but we have a different function. In marriage the husband and wife in essence share responsibility for the success or failure of their relationship but in function. The husband has the responsibility to lead the family in the direction God has ordained and the wife's function is to support her husband in his godly endeavors. Consider the following: a chicken is either a rooster or a hen. Roosters and hens are not confused about their sexuality. Roosters instinctively know they are to rule the roost and hens instinctively know that they are to incubate their eggs and care for their chicks. God has declared the distinct gender differences in nature, which confirms His word. Therefore the spiritual connection that God intends for marriage can only occur between a man and a woman.

Domestic Partnership

The radical gay rights community advocates domestic partnership as a means of publicly advancing their homosexual agenda. A domestic partnership is a same sex relationship where the people involved seek legal recognition of their relationship similar to a marriage. This legal recognition would give domestic partnership all the privileges and benefits of a marriage. Although homosexual couples can have a soulish and physical connection they cannot have a spiritual connection because God does not ordain homosexual relationships. God loves unconditionally and He provides grace and mercy for all but He does not sanction any relationship that is contrary to His Word. Homosexuality can no more be blessed by God than adultery because God's original intention for marriage was monogamous which is one man united with one woman for life.

What do you say to those who say we should legalize same sex marriage as a remedy to the over 50% divorce rate? A good response would be that you do not legalize murder because people are killing one another. In God's omniscience He has established that premeditatedly taking someone's life with malice and aforethought is wrong. In the same way God has established that sexual relations between same sex partners are wrong. Lucifer was God's greatest creation before his rebellion against God. He seduced one-third of heaven's angels to rebel with him; now that he is cast out of heaven his name has been changed to Satan. Satan and his demons are envious of the fact that when men and women come together under the headship of Christ they not only have the potential to be spiritually connected but they are in the image of God. Satan knows that he cannot destroy God therefore he seeks to destroy God's image by undermining the family. Satan will use whatever strategy that is available to destroy the image of God whether it's killing unborn babies through abortion, causing contention in marriage that results in divorce, or leading us to believe that homosexuality and heterosexuality are the same. We must not be ignorant of Satan's devices, which mean we should stand against any method Satan uses to attack the image of God.

Some homosexual couples desire to change the definition of marriage from its legal union of a man and a woman to the legal union of a same sex couple. Cultural norms are changing where what was unacceptable ten years ago is acceptable today. It is important to understand that although cultural norms change God's intention for marriage has not changed because He is immutable and His truth is not subject to change. A father can no more change himself into a mother than a mother can change herself into a father because that type of change would be contrary to nature. Both God and nature agree that you are either born a man or a woman. Therefore when homosexuality is present it can be the result of a generational habit passed from one generation to another, it can be the result of some psychological trauma, or homosexuality can be caused by the influence of social factors. Once we recognize the source of the problem we can petition God for deliverance and seek God for the grace that will be necessary to repent of that lifestyle. When the change of lifestyle takes place the individual's spiritual connection with God can be restored. Once an individual is free from their homosexual past they can pursue marriage as God has ordained it.

Unity in Worship

When a married couple worships in unity they position themselves to experience their spiritual connection with God together. In I Corinthians 7:15 we are told that the believing spouse sanctifies the unbelieving spouse. Sometimes unbelievers marry and later in life one or the other accepts Christ. Under these circumstances there will not be a unity in worship because the unbelieving spouse cannot experience God in His fullness. However, if the believing spouse prays for the conversion of their unbelieving spouse and walks in integrity God can move on behalf of the relationship. The believing spouse needs to ask God for the grace to maintain their marital responsibilities in joy so that the unbelieving spouse will be converted by their lifestyle. God has called the husband to be like Christ and the wife to be like the church. In the same way Christ provides loving leadership for the church so should the husband provide loving leadership for his wife and family. When a woman finds herself in this position of leadership she needs to pray for her husband's strength in the Lord and encourage him to grow in the things of God. In this situation there is likely to be a challenge when the husband matures and begins to walk in his God ordained authority. The wife in this situation should try to practice humility and encourage her husband to take the spiritual lead in the relationship. The husband should try to ask God to provide wisdom in how to exercise his newfound authority and both parties need to be patient in this transition.

Although I was serving in ministry while I was married I failed to pray and study God's word with my wife on a regular basis. My failure to maintain a regular spiritual devotional time undermined the spiritual connection in our marriage and subsequently led to the demise of our relationship. Unity in marriage also includes the husband taking lead in designating a devotional time for the family. There is an old saying that says, "A dog only looks up when it has rained or when it's on its back." In other words the husband should not wait for a crisis to occur before he looks to heaven and pray. Hopefully husbands will have individual devotional time as well as devotional time with his family. Well what is the wife supposed to do if her husband does not lead the family in regular devotional time? Of course she should ask God to turn her husband's heart toward building the spiritual connection in their relationship but she should also personally encourage him to take the lead. The wife can gently suggest that they spend more time in spiritual devotion by asking her husband in a soft tone, "Can we spend some time next week praying and studying together?" She needs to pay special attention not to nag or pressure her husband. This is important because we never want to use the flesh to accomplish a spiritual objective. Rather than putting undue pressure on her husband the wife may need to take the responsibility of handling the spiritual devotion for her family until such time as her husband steps up to the plate. Perhaps you are thinking you don't have time in your busy schedule for spiritual devotion. Have you ever heard the saying, "For time you must make time?" We have time to do what we think is important, we make time to brush our teeth in the morning, we make time to go to work, we make time to eat and we make time to sleep, therefore we can make time for our spiritual devotion.

Private worship occurs during out devotional time but public worship occurs when we go to church and experience God with other believers. Under ideal circumstances the husband and wife should worship God in the same church. This aids the couple by solidifying their spiritual connection because it becomes likely that they will discuss the messages they receive as part of their spiritual devotion. Not only is it a good idea to attend service together but if there is an area of ministry where they can serve together this can also facilitate their spiritual intimacy. Since the husband is the head of the family the wife should be willing to submit and follow him wherever he believes God is leading them to worship as a family. We do not live in a perfect world and sometimes the wife might not be willing to follow her husband to another church. If this is the case a wise man would not demand that his wife submit to him autocratically because this is likely to cause her to dig her heels in deeper. He should discuss the reason for the change with the wife and ask her to trust his judgment. If she still refuses to go with him he should respect her decision and go by himself. Husbands need to be mindful that the law of love is greater than the law of submission. A man must love his wife even when she is not willing to submit to his authority.

It is important to note that even though the husband is mandated by God to be the spiritual head of the household, he is not always right. It is possible that the wife may be convicted that the family is worshiping in the wrong place. If this is the case the wife should speak with her husband after she has asked God for wisdom in the matter. Perhaps the couple can compromise and visit both churches until God gives them peace about where they should worship together. Under no circumstances should either spouse attempt to force their choices on the other. If there is an impasse in any area that affects their spiritual connection and those issues cannot be resolved through fasting and prayer they should be discussed with an objective person who can offer godly counsel. This person can be a family friend, a member of clergy, or a professional counselor. If you are married you should strive to maintain your spiritual connection through the unity of worship because this will facilitate intimacy in the soulish as well as physical connection of marriage.

Unity of Calling

When a married couple shares a sense of purpose together and they feel led to walk together in the same direction they have a unity of calling. In Genesis 2:18 God makes clear that it was not His intention for man to be alone therefore He will provide help for him in the areas where he is deficient. In essence a man's wife is called to help him fulfill his divine purpose. Does this mean if a man is a corporate executive his wife should be his secretary? Does this mean if a man is a professional athlete that his wife has to be his manager? No, but it does mean that marriage is intended by God to be a team where both spouses have responsibility to accomplish a specific purpose together. Marriage is a calling, by this I mean that the couple senses a magnetic connection to one another that transcends their natural feelings. When they examine their sense of connection separately and together they realize that they are together for something bigger than themselves. The purpose for which they are together facilitates their spiritual connection and they sense they are closer to God because of their unity of calling. Whatever their calling together is they cannot fulfill it in its entirety by themselves. The calling may be the awesome responsibility of raising a godly seed. God has ordained for strong marriages to be one of the pillars of our society. A strong marriage in Christ will give birth to a strong family. A strong family in Christ will give birth to a strong community. A strong community in Christ will give birth to a strong nation. A strong nation in Christ will have a positive impact on our world. Therefore when a married couple considers the "unity of calling" in their relationship it is important that they understand what they do together has the potential to frame their world.

For a brief season I served in my local church as the Director of our Ministers in Training program. During that time I was privileged to help prepare those members of our church who believed they were called to pulpit ministry. I became very well acquainted with one of the women in the class who had a great passion for the ministry God had called her to. Unfortunately she got married before her ministry training was complete. I saw her many years later and she shared with me how marriage and children caused her to lose focus on her call to ministry. She further shared how she and her husband were not spiritually connected enough for him to understand her purpose. When I looked in her eyes I discerned that she was very unhappy. Even though she was married with children she was missing the unity that comes from a shared sense of calling. I attempted to exhort her by sharing the importance of marriage and her children and I committed to pray that both of them would operate in the fullness of their purpose in and outside of marriage. But what do you do when you have married someone who does not understand your calling? It is important for you to try to share with them the importance of what you believe God has called you to do. Let's say for example you believe you have been called to feed and clothe the homeless. Before you use household monies to fund the project you should get the approval of your spouse. In this way you are showing your spouse respect by sharing with them what you believe God has called you to do. If you cannot get agreement from your spouse to use household monies the next step would be to attempt to raise money for the project outside the home through family friends or colleagues. If money is unavailable it might be necessary to simply volunteer your time. Always remember that next to God your marriage takes precedence over everything that God has called you to do outside the home. If your calling outside the home is in conflict with your calling inside the home you need to have faith that God will create an environment for you to do all He has called you to do as long as you stay within His perfect will.

Often times when we think of God's calling on our lives we think of some great spiritual purpose that is connected with the church. Your spiritual vocation can include such activities as serving in church leadership or taking your ministry outside the church on foreign missions. We must also consider the fact that God can call us to areas that are traditionally considered secular vocations. This can include being a schoolteacher or restaurant entrepreneur. Whether our calling is spiritual or secular in nature the principle of accountability to your spouse remains applicable. It is important that we maintain accountable to our spouses because this lays the groundwork for marital unity in your calling. What if your calling requires you to go back to school? You will need the support of your spouse to pick up the slack in areas that may be neglected such as domestic responsibilities or childcare. There should be a willingness to cooperate with one another so that you can achieve God's call together.

Marriage has many challenges that can lead to divorce such as poor communication, a poor sex life as well as financial challenges but when a married couple has unity in worship and calling they have a spiritual connection that can carry them through the difficult times. Your priorities are out of order if you are investing all of your time and energies in pursuing bigger houses and fancier cars at the expense of the most important component of your marriage, which is your spiritual connection. If you find that area lacking make a commitment with your spouse to change. If your spiritual connection to your spouse is strong be encouraged that you have the foundation for a great marriage.

The Soulish Connection

The soulish connection in marriage occurs when the married couple joins their will, intellect, memory, and emotions together for the purpose of deepening their marital bond. This includes having an open line of communication where they can freely share their thoughts and emotions on any given issue. The soulish connection pertains to the horizontal bond that exists in the couple's personality. Conversely, the spiritual connection pertains to the vertical bond that exists with God, both are essential to a healthy well-balanced relationship.

When we look at David's life we see a vibrant personality. One minute he is defying the Philistine giant, Goliath, and the next minute he is pledging his faithfulness to his friend, Jonathan, proving that David has a soul with great depth. In Psalms116:8 David said of God:

> *For you have delivered my soul from death*
> *my eyes from tears and my*
> *feet from falling.*

David not only had a spiritual connection with God but his entire soul was linked to God, even his thoughts and emotions. Even though David had an excellent relationship with God he still longed for his soul to be connected with others such as Saul, Jonathan, and his wife Michal. In I Samuel 18:28 we are told that Michal loved David. There is no doubt that she was captivated by his personality. David's soulish connection with his wife was distinctly different from the connection with the men in his life. God has created men and women distinctly different. Generally when we think of the differences between men and women we think of our physiological differences. It is important to understand that we also process our thoughts and emotions differently. When these differences are not understood it can hinder the soulish connection that is important for a healthy marriage.

Is it true that women are sometimes confused by the actions of men? Why do men often feel that women don't make any sense? One of the reasons for our gender misunderstanding is because we do not seek to understand before we seek to be understood. By this I mean that since we know more about ourselves than we do others we view their actions from our subjective point of view. If you are wearing yellow glasses and I am wearing blue glasses as long you look at me from your glasses and your point of view I will be yellow. In order to be objective you must take off your glasses and try to put on my glasses and see things from my point of view. My point is that gender misunderstanding is due to our inability to understand the other person from their perspective. This is often a hindrance to the soulish connection within marriage.

Perhaps we can better understand the opposite sex after we review the research of Dr. Roger Sperry. Dr. Sperry was a professor of psychobiology at the California Institute of Technology. In 1981, he was awarded the Nobel Peace Prize for Physiology as a result of his medical research on the brain. Although there are obviously cultural reasons for gender differences in behavior, research shows that many of our differences may lie in our heads. The brain is bilateral with the left side controlling objective, analytical, and rational ability while the right brain controls subjective, emotional, and creative ability. Men are often left-brain dominant and women are often right-brain dominant. The bridge of fibers that separates the left-brain from the right brain is thicker in women than in men. As a result, women often make connections that might not occur to a man. The reason that young girls speak sooner and read faster than boys is directly related to the configurations of their brains. It is believed that although a woman's brain is 10-15% smaller than a man's brain the region's that govern language are more densely packed with neurons, this is perhaps one of the reasons women have such a way with words. Women will sometimes maintain a conversation with questions and when upset they will often desire to release their hostility verbally.

Since men have a tendency to be left-brain dominant their thought process and conversation have a tendency to be linear, words are simply a way to relay information. Conversely, the right brain dominant woman has a circular thought process and conversation is her way to discover thoughts and feelings. Men are often concerned with the big picture and the bottom line of reaching a goal. This makes men task-oriented, which gives them a sense of achievement. Women can be detail-oriented and they often enjoy the process of getting to the goal as well as reaching the goal.

The soulish connection between a husband and wife will be hindered if the man does not understand that most women use conversation to negotiate emotional intimacy. Being best friends to a woman means that you can sit down and talk about anything. When a woman can talk about the things that concern her and she senses she is being listened to she connects and builds a bond of intimacy. Oftentimes men interpret a woman's expression of intimate thoughts as a request for advice. When he hears trouble he naturally responds with a solution if he has one. When a woman continues to share her concerns and doesn't respond to the man's advice, he gets frustrated and confused. He eventually may discontinue responding altogether because he does not understand her indecisiveness. What a man needs to know is that when a woman shares her intimate thoughts and feelings she is often looking for him to reciprocate with some similar concern. If the man understands that sharing a related concern helps establish a sense of emotional intimacy he can go a long way in sustaining a soulish connection with his mate.

The Will

Our will is the faculty within our soul that enables us to make deliberate choices. If a married couple has a pre-arranged fixed budget with all the family's expendable funds in a joint checking account what should the wife do when she desires an article of clothing that is outside of that budget? If she has no other funds outside of the family's joint checking account she should use her will to step outside of her right brain emotional desire for the item. She may also elect to consult with her husband and see if they can make an adjustment in the budget for her. If her husband says no she should will to submit to his authority as head.

In this scenario the husband could will to step outside his left-brain analytical reason for adhering to the budget and make an adjustment in the budget so that he can meet his wife's desires. The couple should will to make decisions that will benefit the family over their individual needs. If they will remain accountable to one another they will be able to avoid many of marriages pitfalls.

Intellect

Our intellect is the faculty within our soul that enables us to think and reason logically. If the husband understands that his wife's right brain makes her very creative he will understand her desire to decorate the house. Rather than get into a contentious argument about paint, window treatments and carpet, the husband should reason with his wife. He could suggest that she decorate the living room, dining room, kitchen, bedroom, and bathrooms, while he decorates the den, basement and home office.

A husband and wife should be able to use their intellect to reason with one another, this spirit of cooperation will help build intimacy and a spirit of teamwork.

Emotions

Our emotions are the faculty within the soul that enable us to sense non-physical feelings. What does a wife do when her husband's child from a previous relationship calls the house to speak to their father without saying hello? If she perceives the child's behavior is rude she should explain her feelings to her husband. The husband should listen intently to his wife's concerns and respond by addressing the issue with his child. He should be mindful of his child's emotions also and communicate to the child the importance of showing his wife respect and courtesy.

If possible it would be wise for the husband to try and bring his wife and child together for the purpose of building an extended family type relationship. The positive feelings that can grow from the extended family relationships can secure the marital bond.

Memory

Our memory is the faculty within the soul that enables us to recall past events. If a husband has pictures of an ex-girlfriend in his photo album it is possible that they will trigger memories of time spent together. He may reason in his left brain that there is no harm but he should consider his wife's feelings over his own.

In marriage it is important for the husband to take the lead this includes him setting aside his past so that he can move his family toward the future.

Imagination

Our imagination is the faculty within the soul that enables us to visualize pictures in our mind. The married couple needs to set realistic goals using their imagination. Imagine what it would be like to be debt free. Imagine what it would be like to be able to resolve all your differences through effective communication and be able to avoid divorce. If a married couple can see their relationship through the eyes of faith they will be able to imagine the best for their relationship. As they strive to meet their goals their intimacy will increase as the accomplishment of one goal leads to another. Even if they fail they still have the ability to hold on to their dreams together. The soulish connection in marriage can be difficult to maintain especially if the components of the soul show a distinction between how men and women process information, is misunderstood. However when the couple keeps God first and considers the other partner's feelings before acting, their relationship has a great potential for success.

The Physical Connection

The physical connection in marriage occurs when the man and the woman are satisfied with the physical aspect of their relationship. This includes the couple finding one another physically attractive along with their need for affection and their sexual desires being met.

We know that monogamy was God's original intention for marriage but during Bible times polygamy was culturally acceptable for men who had great authority and great wealth. David had nine wives and an unknown number of concubines. David had a reputation for being passionate about everything from his relationship with God to his desire to build God a temple. There is no doubt that for David the physical connection in marriage was of great importance. The Bible tells us in I Corinthians 7:2:

> *Nevertheless because of sexual immorality let each man have his own wife and let each woman have her own husband. The wife does not have authority over her own body but the husband does. And likewise the husband does not have authority over his*

own body but the wife does. Do not deprive one another except with consent for a time that you may give yourselves to fasting and prayer and come together again so that Satan does not tempt you because of your lack of self-control.

Biblically, the only legitimate way for a man and a woman to satisfy their sexual desires is within the covenant of marriage. The marriage covenant makes both the husband and the wife accountable to meet the other's sexual desires within reason. There are times when the couple may agree to abstain sexually because they are seeking God in a specific area but neither spouse should make the decision to abstain independent of the other. When there is a physical connection between a husband and a wife and they are satisfied with their sexual relationship there should be no problem in avoiding Satan's attempts at sexual temptation.

What should you do if your spouse is not interested in being sexually intimate with you? That is going to depend on the reason why. Sexual intimacy includes any physical contact that stimulates erotic feelings up to and including sexual intercourse. Sexual intimacy should be a result of the couple being spiritually and soulishly connected. Therefore any lack of sexual interest may be due to the couple neglecting intimacy in the other areas of their marriage. Sometimes that lack of sexual interest may not be due to neglect but it could be the result of physiological problems. Below we will review three common problems men face that have the potential to cause male impotence:

1. Diabetes
   Diabetes is when the blood sugar is elevated above normal levels. The pancreas produces insulin, which regu-

lates blood sugar. When there is insufficient insulin to balance the body's blood sugar it has the potential to cause poor blood flow to the penis which may affect the man's ability to get and maintain an erection.

2. Hypertension
Hypertension is more commonly called high blood pressure. Blood pressure is determined by the amount of blood pumped by the heart along with the size and condition of the heart. Blood pressure is affected by the individual's physical condition, diet, and genetic factors. Hypertension, like diabetes, has the potential to cause poor blood flow to the penis which may affect man's ability to get and maintain an erection.

3. Prostate Enlargement
Prostate disorder occurs when the prostrate is not functioning properly. The prostate is one of the glands located within the pelvic cavity that produces semen. The prostate continues to grow throughout life. Sometimes this enlarged prostate disrupts the man's ability to urinate. Infections and bacteria from other parts of the body can invade the prostrate and cause cancer. Sometimes when there is a prostate disorder it will affect the nerves in the penis, which may affect the man's ability to get and maintain, an erection.

Below we will review three common problems women face that have the potential to cause a lack of sexual desire.

1. Premenstrual Syndrome
    Premenstrual Syndrome is a chronic mood disorder that sometimes precedes a woman's monthly menstrual cycle. Approximately every 28 days the unfertilized egg in a woman's uterus dies and is released in her menstrual flow. Premenstrual Syndrome can be caused by fluctuations in hormone levels, deficiency of certain vitamins and a poor diet. Symptoms such as depression, backaches and bloating are likely to contribute to a woman's sexual disinterest.

2. Post-Partum Depression
    Post-Partum Depression is a chronic mood disorder that sometimes occurs after a woman experiences childbirth. If a sufficient hormonal imbalance occurs after pregnancy along with the overwhelming responsibility of caring for a child depression can follow. Symptoms such as chronic fatigue, poor appetite and irritability are likely to contribute to a woman's sexual disinterest.

3. Menopause
    Menopause also termed "the change of life" is the transitional period in a woman's life where she experiences her menstrual cycle less frequently until

menstruation completely stops. Symptoms such as hot flashes, abdominal pain, mood changes and vaginal dryness are likely to contribute to a woman's sexual disinterest.

If you are experiencing any of the above listed psychological or physiological problems be encouraged help is available. I encourage you to seek the appropriate mental or medical professional for the specific treatment for your condition. There are a host of other situations that occur in married life that could hinder the couple's sexual intimacy such as illness, job distress, and family problems. This is the reason that the spiritual and soulish connection is so important for a well-balanced marriage. When one part of the relationship is weak you can rely on the other parts to carry you through. If sexual intimacy is being hindered for any reason the person who is being affected should ask God for the strength to demonstrate unconditional love until the relationship returns to normal.

It is important to understand that the physical connection in marriage is not just based on sexual intimacy. Non-sexual touching such as hugs, non-erotic kissing, and holding hands are also expressions of affection that can bring comfort in the absence of sexual intimacy.

Have you picked up any weight in the last few years? The answer to that question is probably yes, especially if you have been married over a period of time. It is true that spouses should love one another unconditionally but that should not be used as an excuse not to take care of yourself physically. Maintaining a healthy diet and including weekly aerobic exercise will aid your appearance and can go a long way in maintaining the physical connection in marriage. Consider this: a wife should not cut her hair without first consulting with her husband. Likewise a husband should not grow a beard without first consulting with his wife. We know that the husband has been ordained to be the head of the family but in love he should be just as accountable to his wife as she is to him. If the couple makes a covenant of accountability and love with one another the results will go a long way in maintaining a balanced relationship with a spiritual, soulish, and physical connection.

Summary

David and Michal's relationship was an extension of his ministry relationship with Saul and his friendship with Jonathan. Their story illustrates not only how important people are to our purpose but also how our relationships are often connected to one another.

We know that David and Michal did not date before they got married because dating, as we know it was simply unheard of during biblical times. Nevertheless, if they did date one another, it would probably have been for the purpose of getting acquainted for marriage. In our culture there is so much casual dating that it exposes the parties involved to intimate emotions with different people that should only be reserved for that special someone. Therefore wisdom dictates that committed dating relationships should be reserved for those people that one considers as a potential spouse. In the courtship stage of the relationship marriage should be the objective. It is important that those who are courting have an objective person who can give them counsel about their relationship. This counsel can come from a member of the clergy of their church or a professional Christian counselor outside the church.

One of the primary reasons for difficulty in marriage is that one or both parties fail to maintain their vertical focus on God and His purpose for the relationship. Not only does God give the married couple a sense of purpose together but He also predetermined the roles that the husband and wife should operate in. The husband should be the head and the wife should be his helper in the fulfillment of their purpose together.

God made man in His image spirit, soul, and body. The marital union is at risk of failure when the couple does not attempt to balance their spiritual, soulish, and physical connection. Both the husband and the wife should try to maintain their unity of worship and calling together because this is the foundation of their spiritual connection. If their spiritual connection is in place they are likely to be sensitive to God's leading in their soulish and physical connection. It is inevitable that there will be challenges in marriage but if the couple can keep their focus on God and their purpose together their marriage will ultimately bring God glory.

CHAPTER SIX

Preventing Divorce

꽃

(Principles for a healthy Marriage)

A triangle is a polygon that has three sides, each side is represented by a line that connects to the other two lines at right angles. When you look at a triangle it is plain to see that the bottom line is the base for the other two connecting lines. God intended marriage to be like a triangle with Himself being the base for the husband and the wife who are connected together for the purpose of bringing His will in the earth. The closer the husband and the wife are to God the closer they will be to one another because God is their base and ultimately what connects them together. The base is not only faith in God but adherence to the biblical principles that relate to marriage. There can be no triangle apart from its base, in the same way, apart from God a married couple risk their marriage not being all God intended for it to be. There are secular marriages that survive without God as their base but they cannot experience God in His fullness individually and as a couple.

God is The Father, Son, and Holy Spirit and He made

man in His image, spirit, soul, and body. God has ordained 3 to be the biblical number of completion and His plan is that marriage would be more harmonious as a trio rather than a duet. The success of a husband and wife in marriage is not just a dependent on their connection to God but their obedience to His precepts. In this chapter we will review how we can prevent divorce by paying close attention to the importance of commitment responsibility, financial responsibility, communication responsibility and sexual responsibility.

Commitment Responsibility

Commitment responsibility in marriage is being accountable to God your mate and to the marriage covenant. In I Samuel 18:21, we are told that Saul's motive for giving Michal to David in marriage was to ensnare him with the Philistines. David and Michal's commitment to one another was going to be tested by forces outside their marriage that were beyond their control. Commitment in marriage is important because it is one of the primary ways a couple can overcome the challenges of two people coming together with their idiosyncrasies. David and Michal not only had to deal with their own personal pressures from within but they also had to deal with the external pressures that Saul would place on their relationship. In Genesis 2:24 the Bible says:

> *Therefore a man shall leave his father and mother and be joined to his wife and they shall become one flesh.*

When a man and woman make a commitment in marriage they begin a new family. Next to God all previous priorities and responsibilities become secondary. Although the Bible specifically tells the man to leave his family and cleave to his wife the wife has an equal responsibility to make her family secondary. David was forced to leave

Michal because Saul was threatening his life; in his absence Michal was given to Palti of Gallim by Saul. Michal could have chosen to cleave to her husband but instead she submitted to her father's desire to marry Palti. Saul's interference and Michal's failure to remain committed to her marriage resulted in a divorce.

One of my responsibilities at my local church is counseling. In my experience I have seen the undue influence that in-laws exert on marriage. Sometimes the pressure is so great that the in-laws are more like out laws to the married couple. This is one of the reasons that when I officiate a wedding ceremony I emphasize to the family and friends that marriage begets a new family and that they should make their prayers much and their advice little. What sometimes comes in the form of advice is often meddling, especially if that advice is coming from non-believing family and friends. Family and friends sometimes give advice that is based on what works in their house and not advice that is based on the word of God. Under these circumstances those outside influences can undermine the couples desire to remain committed and their marriage may end in divorce; this can be prevented when the couple gives more weight to their mate's thoughts and feelings than their family and friends.

I am especially empathetic toward people who are going through or have been divorced because of my own personal experiences in that area. One of the reasons my marriage failed is because I did not fully understand the principle of commitment responsibility. Although my divorce occurred many years ago I can recall receiving my divorce papers like it was yesterday. I remember crying like a little baby because I failed God and I felt as if I was an embarrassment to His kingdom. My recollection is so vivid that I would not wish divorce on my worst enemy. I have come to understand that although my divorce was primarily my responsibility God has taken what Satan meant for evil and turned it around for good. I am able to reach those who are having relationship challenges and those who have been divorced. I marvel at how God has used my negative experience for positive results in the lives of so many people.

Divorce

The biblical definition of divorce is the putting away of one's spouse or cutting of the marriage bond. The legal definition of divorce is the dissolution of marriage by the judgment of a court of competent jurisdiction. It is important to remember that marriage is a spiritual relationship that is bound together by the covenant the husband and wife make with God to be faithful partners for life. It is also a secular relationship that is bound together legally by the marriage license which also serves as the marriage contract. Since God is the foundation of the marriage covenant only God can release the couple from the covenant. God intended to keep marriage in tact by biblically limiting divorce to the following two reasons:

- In Matthew 19:9 we are told that divorce is permitted in the case of adultery. Adultery for a married person is considered to be any type of sexual activity with someone who is not your spouse.
- In I Corinthians 7:15 we are told that the believer is not bound to the non-believer who abandons the relationship. Sometimes non-believers marry and one of the spouses accepts Christ when the other does not. In this case the believer is required to stay married because God can use them to convert the unbelieving spouse. If the unbelieving spouse leaves the believing spouse, the believing

spouse would be justified in getting a divorce.

Although adultery and abandonment by a non-believing spouse are technical reasons for divorce it is possible that God will allow those violations to occur and not release the aggrieved party to get a divorce. Sometimes God allows one small thing to precede a bigger thing that is in line with His sovereignty and His divine purpose. God told Hosea to take an adulterous wife who would later have two children that did not belong to him. After Hosea divorced her God told him to reconcile with her because their relationship would be symbolic of His relationship with His people. Obviously nobody wants to be like Hosea but God desires that we keep our marriage commitment because marriages are to be a representation of His relationship with His people.

Does God want us to be foolish? The answer is no. If your spouse is habitually committing adultery or your unbelieving spouse has repeatedly abandoned you I suggest you go to God in prayer and ask Him if it is His will to release you from your marriage covenant. If you are not convicted by the Holy Spirit to stay and you have peace with ending the relationship then do what you believe is right with the mindset that God is your judge.

No Fault Divorce

No fault divorce is the legal dissolution of a marriage when neither spouse blames the other for the breakdown of the marriage. Both spouses agree that irreconcilable differences exist and that they no longer desire to be committed to the marriage. When a couple claim to have irreconcilable differences they are in essence saying, " I don't want to be with you anymore."

Some of the specific grounds for divorce are as follows:

- Irreparable breakdown of the marriage relationship
- Mental incapacity
- Force, menace or fraud in obtaining the marriage
- Impotency
- Willful desertion for one year
- Imprisonment for two years or longer
- Habitual drug or alcohol abuse

In the natural I can understand why a person would want a divorce under the above listed circumstances however none of those reasons are a biblical grounds for divorce. Believers are using the No Fault Divorce laws at the same rate as non-believers because of a lack of commitment responsibility.

In Mark 10:2-9 Jesus was questioned about divorce and he responded that the only reason Moses permitted divorce was because of the hardness of the people's heart. Divorce is a human phenomenon, not a divine one. It was God's intention that the marriages that He ordained would not separate because, "the two became one flesh." Jesus used the "one flesh" metaphor not to indicate that marriage compels a couple to think and be alike in all things but to illustrate the sense of unity marriage should bring to the couple. Once this oneness takes place divorce is devastating because there is a loss of oneself with the separation.

Although there was no such thing as a No Fault Divorce during Bible times, I believe that the same motivation was in place then that is in place now and that is the hardness of men's hearts. Those who insist upon a No Fault Divorce without a legitimate attempt at reconciliation are similar to those in Bible times who would give their spouse a bill of divorcement and in essence say, " See ya wouldn't want to be ya." We have become so unfaithful in our commitment to one another that we forget that as believers we are God's bride and despite all we have done against Him, He has not divorced us.

In Malachi 2:15-16, God says He hates divorce because He is looking for godly offspring. One of the reasons that God ordained marriage was for procreation. God desires to populate the earth with a seed that when that seed is grown to full maturity that seed will serve Him. Parents that are vertically focused on God are critical to this process. Parents are required to train their children with biblical precepts so they can be fruitful ministers of God and productive citizens for the community. When parents fail to keep their commitment responsibility and divorce one another, the children suffer. They suffer because they lack the balance that a father and mother can bring to the household. They suffer because children from divorced households are likely to become divorced themselves. The parents suffer with court visits over *custody and child support.* Court fees can easily range in the thousands of dollars while child support in most states ranges from 20%-30% of the supporting parent's income. Unless the marriage is spiritually, mentally, emotionally, or physically unhealthy it would be best for parents to keep their commitment responsibility because if they do not everyone loses.

Unfortunately when parents divorce they sometimes divorce their children also. It may be due to the custodial parent not allowing the other access to the other parent. Some divorced parents are so bitter that they pass that bitterness on to their children which undermines the relationship with the other parent. Sometimes the lack of child support is not due to neglect or irresponsibility but the loss of a job. If the custodial parent does not understand this they may deny the other parent visitation privileges. Even in the event of a divorce parents need to make an attempt to see that any negative impact be kept to a minimum. The way this can be done is by setting aside your differences and keep a focus on the children's spiritual, mental, emotional and physical well being.

The term "No Fault" divorce for the believer is an oxymoron, by this I mean it is possible to have irreconcilable differences with your spouse but if we take a look within our hearts God will reveal to us how we contributed to the conflict. Therefore before you consider a "No Fault" divorce be honest with yourself and ask yourself why do I want this divorce and is God pleased with my motivation.

Marital Separation

Marital separation occurs when either the husband or the wife chooses to withdraw from one another by living in a different location while remaining married. Marital separation is different from divorce in that it provides for possibility of reconciliation if the reason for the separation is satisfactorily addressed. Conversely, those who divorce generally have no hope of reconciliation therefore they dissolve the marriage. In I Corinthians 7: 10-11 the Bible in essence allows for a marital separation but it admonishes the separating parties to remain unmarried or reconcile with another. God desires to protect the integrity of marriage and He only sanctions divorce under extreme circumstances. Well what about domestic violence? Since God desires that we live in peace I do not believe He wants anyone to remain in a house where there is perpetual physical, sexual, emotional or mental abuse. As a law enforcement official I suggest if you are married and you have been a victim of domestic violence or you sense an eminent threat to your well-being, marital separation may be your best choice. Domestic violence in and of itself does not provide biblical grounds for divorce. If the spouse who has been victimized chooses to separate they should also seek professional help. This help can come from the leadership of your church in the form of counseling or it can come from any of the domestic violence assistance programs that are available in your local court system as well as the community. I admonish you please do not reconcile with your spouse solely based on tears and an apology. If you have a soft heart you may allow your spouse to move back in out of your compassion for them. Tears and an apology are not evidence of a willingness to change. If your spouse is sincere about changing they will demonstrate their commitment responsibility by submitting to a objective person who can be trusted. They should be committed to help both of you toward reconciliation. Reconciliation should only take place after repentance has been followed by actions that demonstrate change.

Once you get a revelation on God's heart for marriage you will understand that unless there exist some aggravated situation, God desires reconciliation for the couple that is undergoing a marital separation. However, if the circumstances that led up to the separation *were* bad enough for the couple to live apart from one another I recommend that they submit to an objective party that has their best interest at heart before they move back in together. This objective party does not necessarily have to be a professional counselor but they should be a mature person who walks in wisdom that both the husband and wife trust. The purpose in submitting to outside counsel is that sometimes the couple is too close to the problem to see the root of the problem. The goal should be to remain accountable to the objective party during the period of transition. After the transition is complete and all parties agree, the couple should reconcile by moving by back in together.

Remarriage

Remarriage is when a person who was divorced decides to marry the same person again or a different person. In Matthew 5:32 we are told that unless the grounds for divorce were adultery to remarry would be an act of adultery. A literal interpretation of this scripture would impact many of the people who seek a "No Fault" divorce especially when the grounds are for irreconcilable differences. God takes the commitment responsibility of marriage so seriously that if you cannot reconcile with your mate you should remain single. I heard someone say, " You can't put a square peg in a round hole." In other words some relationships simply don't fit. What do you do when there is no hope for reconciliation with your ex-spouse but you grow to love another person? In I Corinthians 7:9 we are told that it is better to marry than to burn with passion. Here we have a scriptural paradox and in this situation we may not know what to do. Whenever you don't know what to do ask God for the answer. If you have peace with God about your love for this person, you mutually share a unity of calling and you share a like passion it might be a good idea to get married. Remaining single in this situation may do more harm than good because of the temptations that the mutual passion brings. Marriage under these circumstances should not be based solely on passion but those feelings should be a mitigating factor.

I would not recommend anyone remarry without first getting premarital counseling. The counseling needs to go into great detail about the reasons for divorce. This is important because if you don't find out why you did what you did the first time you are likely to repeat the same mistakes again. Once you have identified the past issues both parties can decide if they desire to move forward. If a person refuses to submit to counseling they may be better off remaining single.

Divorce and remarriage are often the result of either the husband or the wife's failure to keep their commitment responsibility. Although the motivation for many divorces is sinful it is important to understand that divorce is not the unpardonable sin. Wrong motives for divorce can be forgiven and we know that we serve a God of second chances. If through some unfortunate circumstance you find yourself divorced my prayer is that God will show you the reasons for the divorce and if you remarry you will keep your commitment responsibility.

Financial responsibility

Financial responsibility in marriage is being account-able to your mate for the family's money and other material resources. This includes charitable donations, savings, investments and the stewardship of anything of value. In I Samuel 19:12 we are told that Michal helped David to escape the death threats of Saul. Historically, fathers had financial responsibility for their daughters in the absence of their husbands. Therefore, In David's absence Michal only had her father to depend on for financial support until she remarried. Although the circumstances were beyond David's control his inability to maintain his financial responsibility for Michal led to the demise of their relation-ship. In Matthew 6:19-21 we are told:

> *Do not lay up for yourselves treasures on earth where moth and rust destroy and where thieves break in and steal; but lay up for yourselves treasures in heaven, where neither moth nor rust destroys and where thieves do not \break in and steal. For where your trea-sure is, there your heart will be also.*

The material things we value on earth are all subject to deterioration or theft but our true wealth is found in our heavenly investments. Our heart reveals our true attitude about the things that are most valuable to us. Financial responsibility in marriage is a matter of attitude. Sometimes in marriage there is more of an emphasis on material riches than true wealth. This is evident by how many marriages begin. In the United States, statistics show 38 billion dollars is spent annually on weddings and 1 billion on honeymoons. I was amazed to discover that 40% of jewelry sales are on engagement and wedding rings. Engagements, weddings, and honeymoons *are a retail* bonanza due in part to financial irresponsibility. The problem is many people are more interested in investing in the engagement and wedding more than the marriage. The solution is found in getting our financial priorities in order.

What would you do if your spouse said, "My money is my money and your money is my money too?" In the spirit that statement is true because God desires that the couple operates as "one flesh" in marriage. The statement is also true in the natural because in most states the financial and material resources of a married couple are considered to be "community property." Community property simply means in marriage there is no individually owned property, everything of value is jointly owned by both spouses unless there was some type of prenuptial agreement before the couple got married. This is important because if a husband and wife have a different attitude toward their financial responsibility they may be headed for trouble. If the husband desires to invest and save and the wife desires to shop and spend they need to come to a mutual understanding about their financial responsibility. When the husband is a better steward than his wife he can use his biblical authority as head to provide leadership in the area of financial responsibility. However, when the wife is a better steward, she could potentially have a conflict because she is required to submit to her husband. Under these circumstances the wife needs to pray that the Holy Spirit convict her husband of his error and turn his heart toward good stewardship. When the wife does not see an immediate change through prayer she needs to attempt to reason with her husband using facts and figures. Prayerfully God will give her the grace to make a persuasive argument that will convert her husband into becoming a wise steward.

Since the husband is the head of the house, should he handle the finances? It depends on which spouse has more expertise in financial matters. If God blesses me to marry an accountant it is my intention to delegate the financial book keeping to her since that is her area of expertise. I believe that this practice will have the potential of building trust between me and my mate and foster a spirit of teamwork.

Would it be more financially responsible for a married couple to have individual or joint accounts? We have already reviewed that in marriage the couple is "one flesh" in God's sight, this means both husband and wife should have equal access to one another's finances. However in cases of a household where there is only one checking account this may not be practical. Consider this: if the wife is paying the household bills electronically out of the joint checking account and the husband writes a check for an unexpected expenditure there is a possibility that neither party will know the exact balance. Whenever two people are using a joint checking account and the balance is unknown there is a possibility that the account will at some point have insufficient funds. Generally when money is withdrawn from accounts with insufficient funds there are fees attached, which in turn can be the reason for other financial challenges. A recommended solution to this dilemma is to have a joint checking account for household expenditures and the husband and wife can have individual accounts for their personal expenditures. If they agree to deposit their income into the joint checking account and only make withdrawals on predetermined expenditures it will be easier to maintain the account balance. The funds for the individual accounts can be provided from the joint account in a fixed allowance expenditure that is paid just like any other household expenditures. Some married couples have separate checking accounts because they do not trust each other and the different accounts are in place as a contingency for secret activities or divorce. Under these circumstances the challenge is not financial responsibility but the couples attitude toward their marriage. This is a heart issue that may need to be resolved with prayer and counseling. Whatever financial accounting method that is chosen both the husband and wife should keep an open line of communication and make an attempt to be in agreement wherever possible. It is important to understand that the couple has to find a financial plan that works for them and what works for one couple might not work for another.

How does a wife earning more income than her husband affect the household finances? It depends on the attitude of the woman. If the woman believes that her earning power translates into greater authority in the household, there is a potential for conflict. It is not uncommon in our society for women to be more educated and command greater earning power than men. However, a woman's academic or financial status does not change how God views her role in marriage. Although wives are required to submit to their husbands any man who has a wife who has more earning power than he would be wise to be sensitive to areas of potential conflict. His leadership under those circumstances should be preceded with prayer and administered with love, patience, and understanding.

Budget

A budget is a detailed financial plan that estimates income and expenditures over a specified period of time. A swamp is nothing more than a river without fixed boundaries. Often our finances are like a swamp because we have not fixed the boundaries with a budget. Maintaining a budget creates self-discipline through learning how to follow pre-established boundaries. When we maintain a budget our finances can flow freely like a mighty river in the direction we believe God is leading us.

Although budgets are fixed it is important to understand that it is inevitable that unexpected expenditures will arise. Therefore a married couple should plan their budget together and commit to maintaining it. There should be no deviation from the budget unless both the husband and the wife agree. The budget should include the following items: charitable donations, taxes, house hold operating costs, savings, investments, estate planning, and credit.

- Charitable donations for the Christian begin with the tithe. Tithing is the practice of giving 1/10th of your gross income to your local church. Everything belongs to God, therefore to tithe is not only an act of worship but it symbolically demonstrates that the believer surrenders their finances to Him.
  Offerings include whatever you give your pastor or local church above and beyond the tithe.
  Other charitable donations include anything that you give of value to a non-profit agency.
- Taxes are the monies imposed on the public by the government that they in turn will use for public purposes. Taxes range from federal, state, and local income taxes to property and estate taxes. Most employers use payroll deductions as a way of paying their employees income tax but if you are an entrepreneur or self employed you will have to estimate your taxes and set that

amount aside for payment at tax time. Almost all local jurisdictions have a property tax on real estate and some local governments have an annual tax on vehicles that is based on its value.

- Household operating costs include monthly expenditures for food, clothing, shelter, and transportation.
  Other cost include utilities, health & dental insurance, recreation, child support, and other miscellaneous expenditures.

- Savings include the money that you set aside specifically for your short or long-term plans. These plans may include money for family projects or vacations.

- Investments include the monies that you set aside specifically for a long-term gain. Investments differ from savings in that savings are generally for short-term financial goals where as investments are for the future especially retirement.
  Investments may include real estate or any type of property that appreciates in value. Individual retirement accounts, stocks, bonds, and mutual funds are also different types of investments.

- Estate planning includes the money and other resources you plan on leaving behind after you die including life insurance policies.
  One of the most important components of the estate plan is the will or trust. Both

documents indicate how resources are to be distributed upon your death.
- Credit is an amount of money that is borrowed and paid back over time with interest. Credit can be used for anything including homes, cars, and other large purchases.

Would you like to be debt free? Surprisingly enough the answer to that question is not always yes. Many people use credit to live beyond their means. With the exception of major purchases such as a home or car a good rule of thumb is not to use credit for anything you cannot afford to pay off in 90 days unless you are using it for investment purposes. An example of using credit for investment purposes would be to buy property that has been foreclosed. Most foreclosures have equity at the time of purchase. Equity is the estimated value of the property in excess of the liens against it. Most financial institutions only want to be compensated for whatever liens exist on the property plus interest. Therefore, if you can find a financial institution that will give you a line of credit for the purpose of making what ever repairs that are necessary you can sell or rent the properties once the repairs have been made. If the property is rented the monthly rent will give you a positive cash flow. If you sell the property you will be able to cash in on the equity at the time of the sale. With this investment strategy you are using credit to make money.

Another fact that you may not be aware of is that from the creditors point-of-view it is good that you maintain an open line of credit because consistently making timely payments demonstrates that person is a good credit risk. Maintaining good credit is important not only because good credit is a reflection on your name it also is important because life may bring a situation that may require money that you may need to borrow. Good credit is one way to get the lowest interest rate possible. If as a couple, you have bad credit I encourage you to pull your credit reports and develop a strategy to repair your credit. If you cannot do this on your own you may seek the professional help of a credit counselor.

How do you earn your money? Financial responsibility not only includes what you do with your money but how you choose to make your money. Below we will review the four major ways we can earn a living:

- An employee is a person who works for someone and their job is based on the position and not the individual. They are paid hourly or by salary and they may work in the private sector as a factory worker or the public sector as a police officer.
- A self employed person works for themselves and their income is based on their own productivity. They can be a doctor, lawyer or dentist.
- A business owner is a person who engages in a commercial enterprise for profit. They have employees who work for them. The business could be a auto maintenance shop or a retail clothing store.
- A investor is a person who earns a living by providing capital for one or more business ventures. They receive a financial return for their investments a portion of which they live on and the other portion is generally reinvested. The investments could be real estate , stocks, bonds or precious metals.

It is possible you may marry a school teacher or retail sales person who works for someone and they may want to make a change in careers. What do you do if your spouse realizes that your family will have difficulty being financially secure as long as they are working for someone? It is important that both spouses communicate with one another about whatever they are planning. There should be agreement when you are making any type of career change especially if you are going from a salary position to starting a business or making investments. The transition can bring financial hard times which will require emotional support. If the couple can pull together with a common sense of vision the family can benefit in the long run.

The idea of transitioning careers or living on a budget may be overwhelming at first but we have to approach it with a positive attitude. Our family can benefit during a last minute crisis when we have a will or trust established through the estate planning process. Investments and savings help you to go beyond living from paycheck to paycheck while giving you hope for the future. If we are faithful in paying our taxes we have nothing to fear if we are faced with an IRS audit. We always need to remember that we are blessed to be a blessing, therefore a portion of our surplus should go to charitable donations with the tithe being first and foremost. When a married couple is true to their financial responsibility they can eliminate much contention in marriage.

Communication Responsibility

Communication responsibility in marriage is being accountable to express to your mate the thoughts and feelings that are relevant to your relationship. In 2 Samuel 6:16 we are told that Michal despised David in her heart after she saw David dancing in celebration of the return of the Ark of the covenant to Jerusalem. Apparently Michal was offended because as David danced before the people while only wearing an ephod, which is a linen loin cloth. The incident caused Michal to make a sarcastic remark to David and he responded with his own sarcasm. The tone of the communication between David and Michal indicates that there were deeper problems in their relationship. David lost Michal while he was on the run from Saul, but after Saul died in battle he attempted to restore their relationship. Although Michal married another man in David's absence, when David returned for her she had to divorce her husband and remarry David. Perhaps a part of Michal's sarcastic communication was rooted in her reluctance to leave her second husband. Throughout this portion of the narrative Michal is referred to as "Saul's daughter" not as "David's wife." I believe Michal's heart was not with David because she was still "Daddy's girl" and that affection she had for her father caused her to resent her husband. Poor communication is sometimes the result of getting your past confused with your future like Michal did. There are times in marriage when you are unsure where you stand, during those times it is important to pay close attention not only to what is being communicated but how it is being communicated. In Matthew 12:33-34 we are told:

> *Either make the tree good and its fruit good or else make the tree bad and its fruit bad, for a tree is unknown by its fruit. Brood of vipers! How can you being evil speak of good things? For out of the abundance of the heart the mouth speaks.*

The evidence that an apple tree is an apple tree is when it bears fruit there will be apples. Likewise what we say is our fruit. In communication it is important to understand that what is in your heart will eventually come out. There may be rare occasions where individuals will be able to conceal the thoughts and intents of their heart through deceptive communication, but under most circumstances people will communicate their true feelings. Even when a person cannot clearly articulate their thoughts their body language will speak loud and clear.

We not only communicate verbally but we also communicate non-verbally through eye contact, facial expressions and posture. What does it mean when your mate cannot maintain eye contact with you when you are discussing why the bills did not get paid? It may mean that he or she fears your response, or it may mean he or she never wanted the responsibility to pay bills in the first place. What does it mean when your mate has a blank expression when you ask him or her if he or she is contemplating a divorce? It may mean that the love is gone and you need to take action if you want to save your relationship. You cannot fully understand body language apart from understanding the individual. For one person failing to maintain eye-to-eye contact could mean deception, in another it could mean they are serious yet in another it could mean they are simply bored. It is our responsibility to study our mates so that we may understand every facet of their being.

In I Peter 3:7 husbands are told to dwell with their wives with understanding because they are weaker vessels. I think it is interesting that God would call the woman the weaker vessel when a woman has to be physically strong to carry a child for nine months. Not only does she have to endure physical and emotional trauma of pregnancy but she also has to endure a potentially painful child birth that could last anywhere from one to twelve hours. When God says the woman is the weaker vessel, He does not mean that she is less than a man He simply means that the man has the weight of the responsibility in marriage. Sometimes men feel like women cannot be understood; the mere fact God commands husbands to understand their wives is evidence that women can be understood. When I was in school whenever I was challenged by a specific subject, I would make a special effort to study that subject. Although husbands may be challenged by the complexity of their wives' emotions they should take the time to communicate by asking questions about what they do not understand. Not only should husbands ask their wives questions but they also can study them by observing how they handle different situations. It is possible that she favors one child more than another; this may be a reflection on how she was raised as a child. Perhaps she is more interested in going to school than work, this may be an indication that she was unhappy with her current job. When I was married my focus was providing financially for my wife but because I did not study her and I did not know when she was trying to reach out for me emotionally. I have since learned that my ignorance contributed to the failure of my marriage and if I am given another opportunity I will do better.

Listening

Listening in communication occurs when you pay close attention to what is being said. Hearing is simply perceiving sound, but listening goes to the next level of giving careful thought to what is heard. Have you ever looked at someone who was talking to you but you did not pay attention to what they were saying? If the answer is yes you were not listening. One way to determine if someone is listening is to ask them to repeat what you have said, if you don't want to be that direct you may ask them what they think about what you have said. If there are any misunderstandings they can be cleared up at that time. We have previously reviewed that men tend to be left-brain dominant with an emphasis on being analytical and women tend to be right-brain dominant with an emphasis on being emotional. This is important because it will help us to understand why we need different listening skills to understand one another. When a woman comes home from work and says, "I had a hard day at work," if her husband is listening he should understand that there is probably more to what she said than what he heard. It is likely she desires her husband's attention so she can vent her frustration. The man needs to know that his listening is more important than his advice. When a man comes home from work and asks his wife, "are you tired," if his wife is listening she should understand that there is probably more to what he said than what she heard. It is possible that he wants something to eat or perhaps he wants to make love to her. The woman needs to know that her listening and understanding will help her to respond to his needs.

Listening is the responsibility of both the husband and the wife. Practically speaking the man might have to turn off the television in order to listen to his wife and the wife might have to hang up her cell phone in order to listen to her husband. Listening has to become a priority in marriage; which means we will often have to sacrifice some activity or personal time to make our spouse feel that we are listening to them.

Transparency

Transparency in communications occurs when you take the liberty to be honest about your innermost feelings on any given subject. If you expect your mate to be transparent you must attempt to create an environment where they do not feel as if you will judge them if they are vulnerable. This can be accomplished by loving your mate unconditionally regardless as to what is shared in transparency. When the man admits his lack of patience with the children is due to the neglect of his father, the wife should respond by encouraging him to spend more time with the children not by nagging him. Often times when a wife nags in her frustration she creates a greater problem because nagging sometimes inclines a man to shut down. When the wife admits that her disinterest in cooking is due to her fatigue after a long day at work, the husband should respond by cooking himself or by going out to get something to eat. If he demands she maintain her domestic responsibility he will possibly hinder transparent communication in other areas of their relationship.

How many people would you stand in front of totally naked? Unfortunately many married couples feel the need to always wear clothing even in the intimacy of their own bedroom. Transparency in marriage is like wearing little or no clothing. Some people feel vulnerable and ashamed when naked because there is something about themselves that they find undesirable. When people can get naked and look at themselves with no shame, they have come to accept themselves even with their imperfections. The individual must recognize the things they can change and the things they cannot. A woman may not be able to change the stretch marks she received while she was pregnant but she can lose the weight she gained. An individual may not be able to change the fact that they were raised by a single parent and they have no frame of reference on how to operate in a two-parent household. However they can make a commitment with their mate to be the best parents they can be.

If a man were to tell his wife that he found one of the women in his office attractive how would his wife respond? If a woman were to tell her husband she lost her wedding ring how would he respond? The answer to these questions is going to be contingent on the temperaments of the individuals involved. If a husband cannot tell his wife he is being sexually tempted and a wife cannot tell her husband she has lost something of great value they are not being transparent. Imagine what it would be like if you could talk to your spouse like your best friend. Your mate should be your best friend but if they cannot be transparent with you about their areas of vulnerability it is possible they will turn to someone else. If the person your mate can be transparent with is easier to communicate with than yourself it is likely they will become their best friend. If your mate has a best friend other than yourself your relationship is not as strong as it can be. One of the ways to strengthen your relationship is to ask God to heal you of any issues that threaten to hinder your mate from being transparent with you. You will foster greater emotional intimacy if you reciprocate when your mate is transparent with you. If your mate says they are sexually attracted to someone else an appropriate response may be that you have been tempted also but were able to overcome the temptation with prayer and by remembering your commitment responsibility. Transparency in communication helps to facilitate the relationship bond while deepening the emotional intimacy in marriage.

Conflict Resolution

Conflict resolution in communication is the strategy that is used to solve the incompatibilities found within the relationship. When two people come together in marriage there are divergent backgrounds, ideas, interests, lifestyles, and habits that have the potential to cause conflict. Avoiding our issues is like sweeping dirt under the carpet. If we continue to sweep our dirt under the carpet it will eventually make a bulge in the carpet that we will eventually trip over. A successful marriage is not a relationship that is free from conflict but a relationship where tension is resolved amicably by both sides. Have you ever met somebody who was so mean that they could start a fight in an empty room? If that person is your mate you not only need to ask God to change their heart but you also need a strategy for conflict resolution, I recommend the following:

- Pick a time and place where you can discuss the conflict without distraction.
- Attempt to define the conflict from both points of view.
- Recommend and discuss solutions to the conflict.
- Be willing to compromise and agree on solution to the conflict
- Encourage and reward one another as you move toward the solution to the conflict.

It is important to prayerfully take a look within your heart while participating in conflict resolution. This is important because when we do not allow ourselves to feel our emotions we cannot recognize the negative thoughts and emotions that have the potential to sabotage the process. It is possible that your conscious thoughts indicate you want to resolve the conflict but your subconscious memory will not allow you to forget a similar experience you have yet to forgive. If this is the case you must make a deliberate attempt to let go of any yesterday that hinders you from going into your tomorrow.

After you have taken personal responsibility for the conflict open yourself to the fact that any issue can be understood and interpreted in a variety of ways. The recognition that your mate is not you will enable you to begin the process of understanding one another. Recommendations for the resolution to the conflict are likely to result when you are both respectful of your differences. The only acceptable solution is one that considers both points of views as it relates to the will of God. What if the husband and wife still cannot resolve the conflict? Biblically the husband is the final authority in the house under God. A wise man would not exercise that authority autocratically but with love and understanding. This may mean the husband could bring an objective party into the discussion to help resolve the conflict. It must be understood that regardless as to the outcome resolution is not about winning or who has the most power but about unity in the home. The final conclusion to all conflict should be based on the biblical principle that is most applicable and administered in the spirit of unconditional love.

Sexual Responsibility

Sexual responsibility in marriage is being accountable to meet your mate's sexual desires within reason. In 2 Samuel 6:23 we are told that David's wife had no children until the day of her death. David failed to maintain his sexual responsibility to Michal when he withheld sex from her after their disagreement (appropriateness of his dancing before the people). Unfortunately, David did what many married people do when they are upset with their mate. The practice of sexual denial in marriage is wrong because neither mate's body belongs to themselves but to their mate. Some marital partners use sex as a tool of power over their mate, by this I mean if there is something that one partner wants that the other does not, sex is withheld in order to make the non-compliant partner submit. Sex in marriage is ordained by God to be an expression of love and affection not power and manipulation. When sex is used as a tool the motive is always selfish and the practice has the potential to destroy the marriage. If this occurs both parties should ask God to reveal the root cause of the behavior and they should also commit to being sexually responsible to one another. Perhaps you are wondering, "How far do I go in maintaining my sexual responsibility in marriage?" The Bible tells us in Hebrews 13:4:

> *Marriage is honorable among all, and the*
> *bed undefiled; but fornicators and adulterers*
> *God will judge.*

Next to your relationship with God the lifelong covenant union between a man and a woman is the most important relationship we will enter into; it is for this reason that marriage is honorable. Marriage has responsibilities but it also has privileges. One of the privileges is enjoying the marriage bed, which is the pleasure of having sexual relations with your mate. When the Bible tells us that the "marriage bed is undefiled" it is saying that the only way that God considers sex to be pure is between a husband and a wife. The married couple should discuss what their sexual preferences are and if they are in agreement they should feel free to enjoy those activities together. If one partner enjoys oral sex and the other does not that sexual activity should not be forced on the unwilling partner. To force your mate into any type of sexual activity is wrong because force is motivated by selfishness and not love. Sex should not only be motivated by love but by an earnest desire to please your mate. If your mate does not feel as if you love them and you do not have an earnest desire to please them they may feel used and this feeling will likely undermine the emotional intimacy of your marriage.

Commitment Neglect

Commitment neglect results when either spouse perceives there is a lack of accountability to themselves or to the marriage. When a couple feels a sense of commitment in their relationship it fosters a sense of security and stability. Sex involves the expression of emotions as well as physical intimacy. A lack of commitment undermines the emotional desire to have sex with your mate. Under these circumstances this is likely to be a manifestation of a deeper problem. It is possible that the emotional energy that is expended toward the children's issues can contribute to a lack of sexual desire. Sometimes there is more of a commitment to the children than to the marriage. This may be due to the love, affection, and emotional security that is received from the children. If this is the case the couple needs to come together and discuss what they believe will be a solution to the problem. The solution may be as simple as not taking one another for granted and refocusing your affection toward your mate. If it is possible the couple should strive for a "date night" as often as possible away from the children where they can spend quality time together. That quality time should include their favorite recreational or social activity. Giving your mate this type of attention will help create an atmosphere to respond to your mate's sexual desires.

We have previously reviewed some of the physiological reasons that may cause a man not be able to respond sexually to his wife such as hypertension, diabetes, and prostate disorders. A woman's lack of sexual desire could be due to premenstrual syndrome, post-partum depression and menopause. There are other sources of sexual dysfunction such as hormonal and psychological issues. Additionally the use of certain medications can also have an adverse affect on sexual desire along with the use of alcohol and smoking cigarettes. Most physiological and psychological issues that undermine sexual desire are treatable by competent medical and psychological professionals. In our information society ignorance is no longer an excuse for sexual dysfunction, it is just a matter of taking advantage of the options that are available. There is likely to be a period of transition that will require commitment and support. It is important to know that commitment will deepen the sexual enjoyment of marriage.

Financial Neglect

Financial neglect results when either spouse is not a good steward with the family's financial and other material resources. Have you ever heard the saying, " No finance, no romance?" For most of us the answer is probably yes. Finances and commitment in marriage go hand in hand because when they are present they provide a secure environment. Most self-respecting men are going to be mentally affected by the lack of a job or the lack of adequate finances to take care of his responsibilities. With his ego being deflated by a lack of finances he may not be interested in having sex with his wife. Likewise a woman is likely to be emotionally effected by what she may perceive as her husband's inability to provide for his family and therefore lose interest in having sex with him as well.

How much financial security does a woman need? Some would say a little bit more. How much money does a man need to make? Perhaps the answer is the same a little bit more. Sometimes financial neglect is not neglect at all but greed. We often want more then we need and when we don't get it our relationships are likely to suffer. If a woman expects her husband to make a six figure salary when he only had a five figure ability, her greed could cloud her desire for her husband. A man's true value is not found in his bank account but in his character. When a man feels like he has to buy his wife's love their relationship depreciates into a mere financial arrangement. In essence she can become like a prostitute to him.

There should be a balanced pursuit of financial stability that does not exclude either mate's emotional and sexual needs. Sex should never be used as a tool to punish your mate for not performing satisfactorily financially. If there is unemployment or some other area of poor financial stewardship the couple should attempt to find the solution together. The pursuit of the solution has a great potential to deepen the emotional bond, which in turn will make for an enjoyable sexual experience.

Communication Neglect

Communication neglect occurs when either spouse neglects to share the intimate thoughts and feelings that are relevant to their relationship. Do you expect your mate to instinctively know when and how you want sex? If your answer is yes you are neglecting to communicate with your mate. If your doctor does not tell you that he has diagnosed you with cancer you might die prematurely because that information was not communicated to you. You cannot make the necessary changes if you do not know what needs to be changed. Change can begin when you understand your mates love language but before it can be understood it should be explained. If a woman wears lingerie when she feels sexy she needs to make sure her husband understands her meaning. If a man enjoys being touched in a specific place on his body he needs to make sure his wife understands the meaning of his sighs and groans when he is touched there.

It is possible that your mate finds pleasure in something that gives you pain. Perhaps the man enjoys deep thrusts during intercourse but those deep thrust could be painful to his wife. Under those circumstances he should be considerate and ask if what he is doing is causing pain. If the man is not sensitive enough to ask, the woman should try to explain her discomfort. The husband or wife who has an unpleasant odor during sex is probably unaware of the problem, therefore this should be communicated with gentleness and love. The married couples sexual needs are likely to change as the relationship matures. It may be at one point in the relationship they may feel as if oral sex is wrong but as they become more comfortable and more emotionally intimate with one another they may feel that it is an appropriate way to express their love for one another. If this is the case those thoughts and feelings need to be communicated to your mate.

It is true that you have the right to expect your mate to meet your sexual needs but if you nag or make unrealistic demands you may get sex and lose love in the process. We must never lose sight of the fact that our responsibility to love and respect our mate will always be greater than our right to have sex with them. Regardless as to whether there is a commitment, financial, or communication issue it is important to ask God to help you get to the root of the problem so that you can have a healthy sexual relationship with your mate. Not to pay attention to your mate's sexual needs is to leave them uncovered and vulnerable to sexual temptation. The spouse that willfully and deliberately neglects their mate's sexual needs shares responsibility in the event there is an extra-marital affair. Although adultery is biblical grounds for divorce the offended party needs to take a look within their heart and see if they contributed by neglecting the sexual needs of their mate. To seek a divorce for a technical violation of the marriage covenant when you are part of the problem is selfish and self-centered. Under those circumstances forgiveness would be the appropriate response and not divorce.

The loving sexual experiences that are born out of marriage have the potential to connect the husband and wife spirit, soul, and body. The balance of a healthy relationship will not only benefit the married couple but the testimony of their relationship will bring glory to God and be a blessing to others.

Summary

David and Michal's relationship is an excellent example of how a man and a woman can start out standing and end up falling. Saul's interference in their relationship led to their divorce. Marriage has enough internal pressure with two distinctly different people attempting to become "one flesh" hence, it can do without the unnecessary external pressure that in-laws can create. Next to God marriage is our primary relationship. Any relationship that interferes with the primary relationship needs to be closely examined. This includes family and friends, if they do not have a positive impact on the marriage they need to be modified, temporarily suspended, and as a last resort terminated.

In order to maintain a healthy marriage and prevent divorce the married couple should stay focused on their commitment, financial, communication, and sexual responsibilities. There is a risk of a myriad of different consequences up to and including divorce when these areas are neglected. The only biblical grounds for divorce are adultery and abandonment by an unbelieving spouse. God has set the standard for the disillusionment of marriage to be so high because He intends for this relationship to be a living manifestation of Christ and the church. When the church sins against Christ, He does not divorce her but unconditionally loves her back into fellowship with Him. In the same way God expects marriage to be knit together by unconditional love. God hates divorce because it violates covenant and destroys the family unit by not only separating two people who have become one but it is also emotionally devastating to the children who are involved. Divorce is like death without a burial, by that I mean the husband and wife die as a couple but they cannot bury themselves as individuals. Although the marriage is dead they cannot bury the individual thoughts and feelings they have. Those thoughts and feelings can be emotionally devastating, yet as always hope can be found in the life giving resurrection power of God. Even if there is no relationship reconciliation there is life after divorce when we understand that divorce is not the unpardonable sin. Once you have learned from your past mistakes it is time to look to God for the future.

Marriage has the potential to expose the pleasant things you expect such as love, companionship, and understanding, but it also will expose the unpleasant things you don't expect such as selfishness and unforgiveness. God will allow you to see the negative characteristics in your relationship to test the character of your marriage. Will you remain committed or will you give in to divorce? When a couple agrees to remain committed come hell or high water their unity can help them stand against the storms of life. There is likely to be disagreement on how to handle the family's finances, but if the best interest of the family is put forward you can find common ground.

The lack of communication can leave unattended issues that act as termites eating the frame of the relationship unless they are discussed and confronted. Under normal circumstances those conflicts should be able to be resolved by the couple communicating with one another but when they cannot, wisdom says that an objective party needs to be brought in to help.

When there is a deficiency in commitment, finances and communication, sexual expression will also be effected. Sex in marriage is more than a physical act, it is sometimes an outward manifestation of the other inner workings of the relationship. Sometimes marriages face challenges because the couple try to resolve their issues themselves in the natural when the answers they really seek are supernatural in God. As long as we keep God first His purpose will manifest in our relationships.

CHAPTER SEVEN

Motivations For Sex

-ᡰᢱ᠍ᡖ-

(The true reasons we have sex)

For some of us, as long as we have the resources we will attempt to attain the things we desire. If you are hungry what will you do? Perhaps you will get something to eat. If your favorite winter coat is too small and you see another that you like better what will you do? You might buy the coat. If you saw your dream house and it was within your price range what would you do? You may seriously consider purchasing it. Our motivation is due in part to our basic needs for food, clothing, and shelter, but it is important to understand that there is a difference between our needs and our desires. Do you need to have sex? The answer is found in knowing the difference between a need and a desire. A need is a requirement that is necessary for ones well being. A desire is a longing for something specific and is less important than a need. Sex is not a requirement like our primal need for food, clothing and shelter however, our motivation for sex is often based on varying degrees of desire which is often tied to individual preference. In this chapter we will discuss the different motivations for sex: the longing to fulfill physical desires; the longing the fulfill emotional desires; the longing to fulfill paternal or maternal desires; and the longing to give love and comfort unselfishly.

We live in a sexually saturated society. Movies range from hard-core pornography with sexual acts on screen to soft-core pornography with intense sexual themes. Often music has sexually explicit lyrical content whether it be pop, country, or R & B. Written media contains blatant sexual photographs as a means of advertisement and many fiction novels contain vivid lustful themes. Whether it be visual or audible it is difficult to escape the influence of sex in our society. We risk having an unbalanced view of sex if we do not understand what motivates those desires and if we lose focus on God and our purpose.

The Longing To Fulfill Our Physical Desires

The longing to fulfill our sexual desires is a natural motivation that has been given to us by God. In 2 Samuel 11:2 we are told that David was physically attracted to Bathsheba when he saw her bathing from his roof. At this time in David's life he was well established as king. Israel was at war with the Ammorites and David should have been in the field commanding his troops. David saw something he should not have seen due in part to the fact that he was in a place that he should not have been. It is important to understand that being in the wrong place at the wrong time can put you in a position that you may not be able to handle spiritually, emotionally, or physically. When David first met Michal he respected her virtue until they married. Likewise when David met his second wife, Abigail, he respected her virtue also, but when he met Bathsheba something was triggered. Polygamy was the socially legitimate way of men fulfilling their lust with multiple wives during Bible times. Apparently David's basic sexual desires were met with one or maybe all of his wives so what did Bathsheba trigger that his other wives did not? I believe the answer is found in I John 1:16:

> *For all that is in the world the lust of the flesh, the lust of the eyes, and the pride of life is not of the Father, but of this world.*

Lust is the excessive desire for any person, place, or thing that is contrary to the will of God. Desires in and of themselves are not wrong however, when they become excessive and transcend the boundaries that God has established we get into trouble. Lust is not from God but is of this world. The word translated "world" in this passage does not mean the earth, or the planet, that we live on but it is speaking specifically of the people, places, and things that occupy the earth. The world is opposite the Kingdom of God, which includes the people, places, and things that come under the sovereign rule of Jesus Christ as King of kings and Lord of lords.

When David looked at Bathsheba and desired her, he allowed his natural physical desire for sex to become lust. When he allowed himself to desire another man's wife he stepped out of the Kingdom of God into the world. Everyone experiences some form of lust from time to time, but when David allowed the lust of his flesh and the lust of his eyes to motivate him to send for Bathsheba, he missed God. It is possible that Bathsheba was also wrestling with her physical desire for sex. While trying to look at this story from a different perspective I asked myself the following questions, "Didn't Bathsheba know that the king was not at battle with his troops? And if so, why did she bathe outside where she could be seen by the king? Since her husband, Uriah, was at war, how long had it been since her physical desire for sex had been satisfied? Why did she knowingly agree to come to David's home and have sex with him?

Why would she later marry someone who killed her husband?" One can conclude that Bathsheba was lusting also and that she wanted to fulfill her desire for sex with David. I suspect the reason that David responded differently to Bathsheba was due to their common physical desire and lust for one another.

It is possible that David and Bathsheba's relationship involved more than a lust and a physical desire to satisfy one another. We have previously discussed the French phrase, " Je ne sais quoi" which means, "I don't know." It is that something special that makes one person more attractive than another. Bathsheba was the last woman David would have a romantic relationship with and I believe she had that something special. What will you do when your marriage gets stale and you meet someone that has that, "Je ne sais quoi?" It is important to understand that there will always be someone more attractive than your mate consequently there has to be a greater connection between a husband and wife than their sexual desire for one another. Marital faithfulness needs to be sustained with the couples covenant commitment to God and to one another.

During my marriage there were some very intense times when I felt that I was sexually vulnerable. On one occasion I met a fellow female police officer who was not only physically attractive but she had that special quality that made her stand out from other women. She had a warm smile and a pleasant disposition that made her even more attractive. We worked different shifts and I can recall taking time while we were at work to talk. After I recognized how attracted I was to her I discretely discontinued our conversations and just spoke to her in passing. I understood that if I continued these brief verbal encounters it was possible that I could fall into sexual immorality. Although my physical desire to have sex was healthy I understood that God has ordained that any sexual activity outside the bond of marriage is immoral.

Since my divorce I have struggled with the physical aspect of my sexuality as a single man. Saying no to myself, and using self discipline has helped along with staying focused by praying constantly that God ". . . lead me not into temptation." In moments of weakness I have prayed that God would interfere with opportunities to compromise that were present before me and I have watched those opportunities evaporate like water in a glass on a hot day. I have also remained focused on my purpose and have surrounded myself with people who are headed in the same direction. If you are single and struggling with your sexuality, I encourage you to do the same and if you fall, get back up and keep trying until you receive your deliverance. If you are married and are being tempted outside of your marriage I encourage you to avoid getting personal with anyone other than your spouse that you find yourself sexually attracted to. *Please* pray that God strengthen you to remain faithful and discuss your sexual needs with your spouse.

The Anatomy Of Sex

Did you know that different people have varying degrees of sexual desire? This is sometimes due to physiological reasons. The most important male hormone is testosterone. It is not only responsible for motivating the male sex drive, it also stimulates the metabolism. Testosterone helps body hair grow and gives men their deep voice and broad shoulders. In puberty testosterone production peaks and declines shortly afterward. This is why adolescent boys have an increased interest in the opposite sex. With age, testosterone levels decrease along with sexual desire. The female sex hormone is estrogen, it basically has the same effect in women that testosterone has in men. Estrogen production also declines with age and is one of the reasons women go through menopause. If you suspect that you have insufficient testosterone or estrogen your doctor can prescribe hormone therapy to assist in bringing your hormone production back to normal.

Adolescence is a difficult time because during this time a young person's body is developing sexually. Young girls are developing breasts and young boys are discovering the overwhelming sexual nature of their penis. In this period boys and girls may learn to touch themselves in ways to give themselves pleasure, which may lead to further exploration. Masturbation is the process of sexually pleasuring yourself. Masturbation may occur at any age but it is especially common during the adolescent stage. Masturbation is outside the will of God because sexual pleasure was only designed for marriage. Masturbation provides the same sexual arousal as other forms of sexual activity. Anytime sexual arousal takes place a chemical in the brain called dopamine is released. We have previously discussed the fact that dopamine gives a person the feeling of being high. It doesn't take long before you want to feel that high on a regular basis whether you are a teenager or an adult. Testosterone and estrogen create the urge and dopamine facilitates the feeling of pleasure. There is no doubt that the physically and emotionally healthy individual feels better when they are having sex than when they are not. It is possible to get addicted to the sexual experience because of the pleasure that it brings. The only practical way to keep this pursuit of pleasure under control is to teach and practice self-control. Self-control is applicable even if you are married because there will be *times that your spouse* may not be able to respond to you sexually due to physical or emotional reasons. Your unconditional love for one another will sometimes require you to sacrifice your legitimate sexual desires because you have your mates best interest at heart.

Your Erogenous Zones
How do you respond when you are kissed on your neck?

What does it feel like when you are touched inside your thigh? If you are sexually aroused when you are touched in a specific place on your body you have found an erogenous zone. Your erogenous zones are especially sensitive to touch. When touched the nerves in those areas send signals to the brain, which releases dopamine and the feeling of pleasure follows. Foreplay is generally considered to be direct or indirect stimulation of one or more of your erogenous zones before intercourse. Foreplay is often necessary for a woman to be sufficiently lubricated before intercourse. Sometimes foreplay is necessary before a man can get a sufficient erection to have intercourse. Foreplay may include massaging the woman's breast or the man's penis.

The most sensitive area for men is often the penis, which is the male sex organ. When there is visual stimulation or the penis is touched it can become stimulated and engorged with blood. Once engorged with blood it becomes erect. The most sensitive area for women is the clitoris. The clitoris is a small organ that is on the top perimeter of the vagina. Like the penis, the clitoris also becomes erect and engorged when stimulated. The climax of sexual stimulation is orgasm. The man ejaculates semen from his penis and may experience other involuntary muscle reactions such as physical trembling and a warm sensation in his pelvic area. The woman may experience what is sometimes described as an explosion from the inside out to every extremity. A sense of numbness may be preceded by warmth throughout the body. Some women report feeling dizzy and seeing stars. Orgasm releases physical tension, which promotes relaxation and comfort.

Sexually Transmitted Diseases

Although sexual intercourse feels better than putting your hand in a warm glove on a cold day, there are physical consequences to consider if you have sex with multiple partners. The sicknesses that are passed on to others sexually are called sexually transmitted diseases. The following are the most common:

- Chlamydia is a bacterial infection that has symptoms of burning urination, unusual discharge, bleeding, and swelling in the genital area. When treated antibiotics are prescribed. If left untreated it can lead to infertility and pelvic inflammatory disease (PID).
- Genital warts are a viral infection that has symptoms of flat, smooth, or bumpy warts in the genital area. When treated they can be removed surgically or by laser. Once removed they can reoccur because there is no cure. If left untreated they will become uncomfortable but are not life threatening.
- Gonorrhea is a bacterial infection that has symptoms of painful urination and itching in the urethral opening, and abdominal pain. When treated penicillin is prescribed. Untreated it can lead to arthritis and blood poisoning.
- Genital herpes is a viral infection that has symptoms of painful sores and blisters in the genital area. The virus can remain dormant for years without symptoms. Although there is no cure, when treated anti-viral medications are prescribed that decrease viral activity. Untreated it can lead to cervical cancer.
- Syphilis is a bacterial infection that has symptoms of bumps or a skin rash in the infected area. There can be painful urina-

tion and flu-like symptoms. When treated penicillin is prescribed. Untreated it can lead to blindness, psychosis, brain damage, and death.

- HIV/AIDS. The Human Immuno-deficiency Virus and Acquired Immune Deficiency Syndrome is a viral infection that weakens the immune system and has noticeable symptoms of appetite and weight loss, fatigue, diarrhea, and fever. Although there is no cure, anti-viral therapies can be prescribed to reduce the activity of the virus. Untreated, the virus disables the body's ability to fight opportunistic diseases, which can lead to death.

The only fool proof method of safe sex is abstinence. When two parties follow God's model of no premarital sex they will not have to be concerned about pregnancy or sexually transmitted diseases. The use of condoms is not 100% effective in preventing STD's or pregnancy because it is possible it may come off during intercourse. Most condoms have microscopic holes that can allow some bacteria and viruses to enter while having sexual intercourse. It is possible you may be infected with a sexually transmitted disease and remain unsymptomatic for years. You can actually change your lifestyle from one of sexual promiscuity to one of celibacy and not pay the consequences until years later in life. The first thing you need to do is get regular check-ups as a preventative measure whether you are single or married. If you discover you have a sexually transmitted disease you should be honest and tell your partner immediately so they can get medical attention. If the symptoms of a sexually transmitted disease do not manifest until after you are married the newly infected spouse should ask God to give them a spirit of forgiveness and walk in love. When you remain committed to the covenant, God will honor your faithfulness.

The Longing To Fulfill Our Emotional Desires

The longing to fulfill our sexual desires emotionally is one of the ways God has ordained for us to feel love. In 2 Samuel 11:4 we are told that David had sex with Bathsheba after his servants told him she was married. We previously reviewed the fact that David had multiple wives, this would lead us to believe that his motivation to have sex with Bathsheba was more than physical. It appears as if there were emotional desires that David tried to meet through his relationship with Bathsheba. At this point in David's life, he was the number one man in Israel as king, there is no doubt that having that type of power over people's lives was a boost to his ego. We can surmise that David's emotional need to have his ego stroked was met by his sexual conquest of Bathsheba. In Proverbs 16:18 we are told:

> *Pride goes before the destruction and a haughty spirit before a fall.*

You are experiencing pride when you feel that you are better than you really are. Pride leads to destruction because it leads you to go beyond the boundaries God has ordained. In pride all you can see are your own selfish desires. Pride is an emotion that leads to the subtle attitude that you can exalt yourself above the will of God. David's pride not only led him to seduce Bathsheba but when she later became pregnant, it also led him to conceal his sin by arranging for Uriah's death in battle. God responded to David's sin by raising adversity against him from his own family.

Although I have never committed adultery and murder, I can identify with David's desire for women being ego centered. As a young man my motive was to satisfy my physical desires with a woman, but as I matured my physical desires became less important than my emotional desires. If a woman I was attracted to needed someone to light her fire, I would be glad to carry the matches. In my vanity I enjoyed taking my burning desire and setting a woman's soul on fire. There are no words to describe the emotional rush I would receive from hearing a woman sigh or seeing her body tremble. My pride got so great that my primary concern in having sex was the woman's physical response above everything else. I later matured to the point where I did not want a woman's body without the intimacy of her soul and her spirit, which I now know should only occur in the covenant of marriage.

It is possible for a woman to have a bigger ego than a man. Some women use their sexual skills to seduce men into abandoning their relationships with other women. They have learned how to sexually hypnotize men by making all their senses smile. When a woman becomes a sexual expert, her ego is inflated when she can keep a man coming back for more. When she sees that her man is restless in the middle of the night she knows just what to do to put him so sleep. If emotional gratification for having sex excludes love and marriage regardless as to whether you are a man or a woman it will eventually become unfulfilling, vain, and shallow.

Pride is not only an emotional motivation for having sex it is also an emotional motivation for not having sex. Perhaps a married person has a condescending attitude toward single people who are struggling with abstinence. Maybe a single heterosexual person, who is having sex thinks they are better than a person engaging in homosexuality. The single person who has had victory over their sexuality for an extended period of time can get cocky. It is easy to abstain from sex when there is no one around that you are attracted to. That is like not smoking cigarettes when you never liked cigarettes in the first place. The underlying emotion in these scenarios is pride. The married person needs to have an attitude of humility considering how vulnerable they would be sexually if they were not married. Likewise the heterosexual person needs to have an attitude of humility considering how vulnerable they would be if they were molested as a child and seduced by a homosexual at a very young age. Sexual purity is corrupted when it is motivated by pride. Each of us should humble ourselves, understanding that under the right set of circumstances any of us could fall and it is only God's grace and mercy that keeps any of us standing.

There have been times when both my physical and emotional desires for sex were so great that I have cried out to God to remove them but His response is always "my grace is sufficient for you." I have come to realize that the same sex drive that was a source of my pride has now become the source of my humility. Those who have strong sexual desires must realize that God may not deliver you from those desires because by allowing them to remain He can keep you in a place of utter dependence on Him.

Imagination and Fantasy

One of the components of our soul is the imagination. Within our imagination we have the ability to create pictures in our mind of whatever we can conceive. If what we conceive is within the will of God, it is a healthy imagination, but if it is outside the will of God, it is a fantasy. If a woman is at work and during her lunch break she begins to picture preparing a candle lit meal, running bath water, and wearing her husband's favorite lingerie for an evening of love making, this represents a healthy use of her imagination. However, if a man reads sexually explicit magazines along with watching pornographic movies and he begins to conceive how he can apply those techniques to someone he is not married to, this is a fantasy and an unhealthy use of his imagination.

What we imagine and fantasize is a reflection of what is deep within our thoughts and emotions. The last time your mate closed their eyes and kissed you, what were they thinking about? Were they imagining a deeper loving relationship with you or were they fantasizing that you were their favorite actor or actress? The imagination is a very important part of good sex. Most people will not have sex with someone they cannot conceive in their mind's eye, before hand what it would be like. Creative mental pictures while having sex add more depth to the sexual experience. The challenge with our imagination is that we can physically be with our mate but mentally and emotionally be with someone else. Entertaining sexual thoughts of someone other than your spouse is committing spiritual adultery. Likewise, the single person who is abstaining, but regularly visualizing themselves having sex is committing spiritual fornication. The answer to an overactive imagination is to focus on God and His word. Illicit thoughts will fade if they are not fed by meditating on them.

Soul Ties

A soul tie exists when your will, intellect, emotions, imagination, and memories are intimately connected to another person. Below I have listed some of the ways that you can know if you are soul tied:

- Are you experiencing a yearning from within to be with a person?
- Do you find yourself thinking about this person all the time?
- Can you see their face before you even when they are not with you?
- When you close your eyes do you see

yourself with this person?
- When you are with this person do you
sense a strong connection and bond?

If the answer is yes to more than one of the above listed questions and you have had sex with that person you are soul-tied to them. Sex is more than a physical act, it includes your will to choose, your intellect and reasoning for the choice, the emotions you feel, the imagination of what it would be like, and the memory of the experience when it is over. One of the reasons God has only ordained sex for marriage is because the connection of the soul tie creates a bond that is very difficult to break. When adversity faces a married couple they not only have the covenant they made with God holding them together, they have their other responsibilities (i.e. children), and the power from their soul tie keeps them bound together.

Sex between people who are not married can create problems you did not bargain for. Your soul takes a photograph of the soul of the other person you are having sex with. The more people, the more photos in your soul. Unfortunately, in our sexually promiscuous society many of us are walking photo albums. This creates a problem when there is a decision to discontinue the promiscuous lifestyle. Whether you are alone or in a relationship you are likely to be bombarded by images of those past sexual encounters. This can be resolved by renouncing all illicit soul ties in prayer and repenting of the behavior that gave birth to the soul tie in the first place. Our soul ties with those people in our sexual past need to be replaced with our soul tie to God. We have a natural thirst for God that can only be satisfied through fellowship with Him in worship and meditation on the word.

Soul ties in our relationships are not just a product of sexual intimacy they are also a result of emotional intimacy. The soul tie is one of the components of sex addiction. Sex addiction is the result of repeated sexual behavior that over time becomes a pattern and later develops into a habit. The sex addict not only enjoys the physical pleasure of sex but they become emotionally dependent on sex to comfort areas of their life that they are having difficulty dealing with. The sex addict uses sex like alcohol or drugs and the sexual experience has the same intoxicating effect. Sex becomes a bad habit for the sex addict that can be broken through asking God to help you transition to a healthy habit when the sexual urge hits. The replacement activity should be something spiritual like prayer, studying the word or meditating on God. Other activities include exercise or engaging in a hobby such as sowing or carpentry. If you cannot handle your sex addiction on your own you should seek professional help or a support group that you can remain accountable to.

In order to get delivered from your soul tie you may need to do more than renounce the past behavior in prayer. It is also important to change the people you fellowship with. Consider this: if you go for a walk with someone you will either walk at their pace or they will walk at your pace. We should make a conscious effort to walk with those people who are walking with God and ask God to give you the grace to keep up with them according to His will and purpose. Soul ties with people that God has ordained will lead us to have a more intimate relationship with Him.

Sex Crimes

A sex crime is any illegal activity that has sex as an element of the offense. Sex crimes such as prostitution or rape are not motivated by physical desire, a desire for children, or for love but out of a warped emotional need for power, control and sometimes monetary gain. Sex crimes include but are not limited to :

• Prostitution which is considered to be

any sexual activity that is engaged in for money. This includes escort services where individuals will pay for the company of someone for a social engagement that later includes some form of sexual activity.

- Indecent exposure which is considered to be any lewd act or offensive display of the body in public. It includes any sexual acts that are likely to be observed in public.
- Sexual harassment which is considered to occur when an employer or employees harass an individual through intimidation, insult, or ridicule because of gender. It also includes an individual seeking sexual favors as a condition of employment.
- Child molestation and pedophilia are considered to be any sexual activity with children. This includes incestuous sexual activity between relatives.
- Rape and sexual assault are considered to be sexual activity without consent or by force or threat of injury. This includes statutory rape, which is sex with a person under the age of consent. In most states you cannot legally give consent for sex until you are sixteen (16) years old. Date rape is sex with a social companion against their will. Marital rape is sex with a spouse against their will.

There are many factors to consider when trying to understand rape as a crime. In statutory rape it is important to understand that although the victim may have the physical appearance and intellect of an adult they cannot legally have consensual sex until they reach the age of consent. The age of consent varies from 14-17 depending on the jurisdiction. Date rape occurs when a social companion desires sex but will not take "no" for an answer. In some date rape cases alcohol or drugs are used to lower the inhibition of the victim. When alcohol or drugs are used in rape cases they have the potential to take away the victims ability to give consent. Rohypnol is considered by many to be the "date rape drug." It is an illegal sedative that lowers inhibitions and is reported to be stronger than Valium. When mixed with alcohol its effects are devastating. There is much more controversy surrounding the issue of marital rape. Biblically neither spouse should deny sex to the other, however the fact that you are married does not guarantee consent. Sex between married people should be predicated on love, not force. In the event you are raped or know someone who has been raped they should do the following:

- Contact the police to report the crime
- Do not wash or clean up to aid in the preservation of evidence
- Go to the hospital for an examination immediately
- Contact your local rape crisis center. Stay accountable to your counselor or a loved one for emotional support during the healing process
- Give careful thought to the prosecution of the perpetrator. Prosecution may be the only way to obtain the emotional closure needed after such a traumatic event and keep the perpetrator accountable for their actions

Prayer is the supernatural way to face the challenges of life. We know that prayer changes things but in the area of sex crimes under most circumstances we will need to face those issues in the natural to prevent its occurrence in the future. This means keeping the perpetrators accountable through prosecution and counseling. Likewise the victims of sex crimes should attend counseling. The counseling can either be provided by a qualified member of the clergy or a certified Christian counselor.

The Longing to Fulfill Our Paternal & Maternal Desires

The longing to fulfill our paternal or maternal desires is part of God's plan for procreation. In 2 Samuel 11:5 we are told that after David sent for Bathsheba and slept with her she got pregnant. Bathsheba's pregnancy set a chain of events in action that would eventually lead to murder. Bathsheba's husband, Uriah the Hittite, was a soldier in David's army. David sent for Uriah, who was deployed in battle at the time Bathsheba got pregnant. David's intention was to cover his sin by getting Uriah to sleep with his wife while he was on leave. Uriah was a noble man, and refused to have the pleasure of his wife while his soldiers were still in battle. Since David's plot failed he had Uriah re-deployed into battle. David later ordered that Uriah be sent into the heat of the battle where he knew he would be killed. After the death of Uriah, David took Bathsheba as his wife. We cannot be certain as to what Bathsheba's exact motive was in having sex with David, but it is possible that she was also driven by her maternal desire since she had no children. In Genesis 1:28 we are told:

> *Then God blessed them and God stated to them, "Be fruitful and multiply, fill the earth and subdue it, have dominion over the fish of the sea, over the birds of the air, and over*

every living thing that moves on the earth.

God crowned His creation on earth by creating man in His image. God's intention was that man would have dominion over the earth, but since He created only one man and one woman, He had to put in them a desire to procreate. Procreation is God's way of reproducing His image on earth. Father's desire to pass their legacy on to their sons, and mother's desire to nurture their daughters, but God's intention in childbearing is far greater. God's omnipresent Spirit is everywhere on earth. God desires more than a spiritual presence on earth but a natural presence. This can best be accomplished through godly parents having godly offspring that will have dominion in the earth.

I have been a witness of the power of both a man's paternal desire and a woman's maternal desire. One of my greatest joys has been watching my son grow and mature into a young man. As I approach 50 and my son has graduated from college, I have lost the desire to have any more children. On one occasion, I shared the fact that I was considering getting a vasectomy with a female friend and she became very disappointed. I began to ponder her response and it occurred to me that my plans for vasectomy could disqualify me as a potential mate because one of her greatest desires was to bear children. I began to reflect on many of our conversations and I recalled she spoke frequently about marriage and motherhood. It occurred to me that many of the women I come in contact with have strong maternal desires. As strange as it may sound some women want children more than they want a husband. I can recall on one occasion meeting a woman who was very warm and amiable; very early in our initial conversation she asked me if I wanted children. After I explained my situation she turned and walked away from me without saying goodbye. In all fairness, I have encountered some women who didn't have a strong maternal desire, sometimes this is due in part to previously experiencing the joy of childbirth or as they have approached 40 they have lost interest. Likewise, most of the men I know have a paternal desire that is based on their current situation. If they are under 35, with no children, there is generally a desire for children, and if they are over 35, with children, the paternal desire has sometimes depreciated.

Sometimes people get married without discussing the importance of childbearing. This is unwise because the decision to have children is one of the most important decisions a married couple will make together. If you are married and have not discussed this issue with your spouse I admonish you to do so. It is possible that one spouse will want a large family and another will want a small family. Wherever possible there should be compromise without one spouse usurping their will over the other. If you are single and by some unfortunate circumstance you find yourself pregnant your primary responsibility becomes the child despite the status of the relationship. Men should make every attempt to provide emotional and material support for their children. The court should not have to mandate support, it should be the natural response to being a parent. Either party which has unresolved emotions about their relationship should be mature enough to make every effort to set their emotions aside about the success or failure of the relationship and make an attempt to work as a team for the good of the child. The courts should be the final remedy in child support and custody issues when the parties involved cannot resolve their issues themselves.

Contraception

Contraception or the use of birth control is the deliberate act of avoiding the conception of children. There are varying opinions in the Christian community about contraception.

Some believe that birth control is mans way of artificially interfering with God's natural process. They believe we should just let God have His way. Their line of thinking is if God allows you to get pregnant, He will make a way for you to provide for your children. Others believe that God has given us wisdom and common sense to use contraception as a legitimate means of family planning. The Bible does not specifically address contraception and since it is not clearly immoral, illegal, or unethical, it is a matter of conscience. If the Holy Spirit does not convict the married couple that contraception is wrong they should feel free to choose the following common methods of birth control:

- Oral contraceptives, more commonly called birth control pills, contain hormones that prevent a woman's ovaries from releasing eggs during fertilization. There can be side effects such as headaches, nausea, vomiting, and weight gain.
- Barrier devices include male and female condoms. These devices are made of rubber, latex, or polyurethane which trap the ejaculate in the condom. They should be disposed of after each sex act. The female condom, which is composed of two flexible rings; one that is placed over the cervix to prevent entry of the ejaculate, while the other protects the exterior genitals. The male condom is put on the erect penis before intercourse. The diaphragm is a dome-shaped latex cup that is inserted into the vagina before intercourse with spermicide, which is a chemical formula designed to kill sperm.

The diaphragm is designed to cover the cervix so that sperm cannot get into the uterus.

- Coitus interruptus occurs when during intercourse the man withdraws his penis before he ejaculates so that his sperm does not enter the uterus. The problem with this method is that there is sperm emitted in the man's pre-ejaculate fluid, therefore it is not very effective.
- The rhythm method of abstinence is practiced when the couple does not engage in sexual intercourse during a woman's fertile period which is approximately 5 days out of her 28 day cycle.
- Sterilization for men is called a vasectomy. In this procedure the tubes that carry sperm are surgically cut in two and sealed. Sterilization for women is called a tubal ligation. In this procedure the fallopian tubes are surgically cut in two and sealed. Both procedures should only be considered if the couple is certain they do not want to have any more children. These procedures can be reversed but have a very low success rate.

There are other methods of contraception that can be researched by a married couple. Before a married couple considers a specific method of birth control they should pray and consult with a doctor about which method is best for them.

Abortion
Abortion is the termination of an unborn child's life for

physical, health, emotional, mental, or economic reasons. In the 1973 landmark case of Roe vs. Wade, the U.S. Supreme Court ruled that women have the fundamental right to abortions. Although abortions are legal in the United States that does not necessarily make them moral. In the 1940's German doctors legally killed Jews, homosexuals, and mentally disabled persons through state-sanctioned medical experiments. Although this practice was legal in Germany it was illegal in the United States. Laws are subject to change but morals are based on God's truth which is immutable. There are 28 states in the U.S. that have enacted Feticide laws. In essence Feticide occurs when an unborn child is killed due to a deliberate violent act of another human being. The father of an unborn child can assault the mother and if the unborn child dies he has committed an illegal act and can be charged with Feticide. However, a mother and an abortion doctor can terminate the life of that same unborn child legally. This legal paradox illustrates that unborn children are considered to be human and have great value.

The two basic positions in the abortion issue are pro-life and pro-choice. The pro-life position advocates that both the sperm and egg are alive and when they are joined together in conception they become human. At conception the unborn child grows from an embryo to a fetus and he or she has a unique DNA code, which will remain with them throughout life. The fetus is considered to be viable at 3 months of age because he or she is capable of living outside the mother's womb. The pro-choice position advocates that the fetus is not human until it is born. It is believed that reproductive freedom is a fundamental right that helps ensure children will be wanted and loved. There are several methods of abortion. In the suction aspiration method, a vacuum tube is inserted in the vaginal canal, the power of the suction rips the fetus apart and out of the mother's womb. In the salt poisoning method, a salt solution is injected into the mother's abdomen and poisons the fetus as well as inducing labor. Sometimes the fetus is born alive. Women who have undergone abortions not only suffer emotional trauma but they have increased chances of premature delivery, miscarriages, and infant death due in part to the scarring that abortion causes in the uterus.

There are those who feel that the primary difference between an unborn and a newborn baby is its age and where it lives. Unfortunately, the abortion issue is not that simple. What does a woman do if she gets pregnant as a result of rape or an incestuous relationship? What does she do if having her pregnancy puts her life at risk? The primary principle in the pro-life doctrine is that life begins at conception; therefore abortion is ending a life. If we follow this principle to its natural conclusion the only time abortion would be legitimate is if the pregnancy puts the life of the mother in jeopardy. If I had to choose between my wife and my unborn child, I would choose my wife because our marriage covenant should take precedent over our paternal and maternal desires. If a woman gets pregnant due to rape or incest there will no doubt be emotional trauma associated with carrying the unborn child, however, the unborn child is an innocent victim and should not lose its life due to the forces beyond its control. Who knows if God ordained that child to become a doctor, a lawyer, or president? If a child is unwanted for any reason adoption should be considered before an abortion. Abortion is not just an issue for the mother of an unborn child, the father also shares responsibility when he does nothing to save the life of his unborn child. If you are considering an abortion, I urge you to ask God to reveal to you how precious the lives of the unborn are. There are many non-profit organizations and governmental agencies that provide counseling and assistance for those who need help. If you are a woman or man that has had an abortion experience it is important for you to know that abortion is not the unpardonable sin. I encourage you to confess your sin before God and ask for His forgiveness. If you are suffering the emotional trauma of an abortion, pray that God heal your heart and if you cannot get any relief it would be wise to seek the professional help of a Christian counselor.

Infertility

Infertility is the inability of a man or woman to produce offspring. In men it can be due to a low or absent sperm count and in a woman it can be due to an abortion or other health issues. Contemporary medical research has provided many infertility treatments for both men and women including hormone therapy. Progesterone replacement can significantly increase the probability of pregnancy but there are also risks such as unusual bleeding, headaches, and nausea that may complicate the benefits of treatment.

Other assisted fertility methods include *in vitro* fertilizations where a woman's eggs are extracted and mixed with a man's sperm outside her body. This procedure occurs within a specialized cylindrical container, which is where we get the term "test tube baby". The external fertilization process takes place from 6-8 weeks after which the fertilized egg is returned to the uterus of the mother to complete the birth process.

Another fertility method is artificial insemination, the process where sperm or eggs are collected from healthy donors and inserted into the uterus of a woman by a straw-like device. Sperm and egg banks are operated by agencies that specialize in infertility solutions. Donors subject themselves to rigorous medical examinations to determine if they are in good health. Healthy donors who meet the agency's profile are paid between $500.00 - $5,000.00 depending on their contractual agreement with the agency. The sperm or egg is preserved for approximately 6 months to test for infectious diseases after which it is used by clients who are satisfied with the profile of the donor.

Christians who consider assisted fertility methods such as *in vitro* fertilization and artificial inseminations may face ethical questions as to whether they should go to these extremes in meeting their paternal and maternal needs. As with the use of contraceptives there are varying opinions within the Christian community about the use of assisted fertility methods. Since the Bible does not specifically address the issue it is a matter of conscience. Each couple should pray and ask God to uncover their motives for wanting children and why they believe the method they have chosen is best for them. Another important fact to consider is the cost of these procedures. Each couple has to prayerfully determine if the expense involved would be the best example of good stewardship.

Adoption and Foster Care

Adoption is the legal process that qualified adults go through to get custody of a child that is not theirs biologically. Foster care involves the care taking of a child who is in the custody of state qualified adults. Although child bearing and parenting are legitimate desires which are given to some of us by God, everyone is not physically capable of having children. Sometimes those who can have children are not mentally, emotionally, or financially capable of caring for them. It is possible that an unborn child may be unwanted for purely selfish reasons. Under these circumstances adoption or foster care are legitimate options.

Most people consider adopting newborns, however adoption services are available for children of all ages. Each state and local jurisdiction has a legal process for adoption. The process can begin through a government funded social service agency or a private adoption agency. If a private adoption agency is used they must be licensed to operate in your state. The adoption service will operate as a liaison between the child, their family, and the perspective adoptive parents. The adoption process will include the following:

- Pre-adoption consultation for the parents involved
- Medical evaluation for the child
- Psychological evaluation for the child
- Educational assessment for the child
- Family therapy including parent coaching and support

The perspective adoptive parents must also undergo a home study report, which is required before the court will grant the adoption. The home study report will help the court determine if a stable home environment exists for a family to receive an adoptive placement. The home study report will include:

- Criminal history check
- Employment status
- Emotional well being of parents and other children in the household
- Overall household environment including the residence and community lived in

All adoptions have fees that range from $5,000.00-$50,000.00 depending on the pre- and post- adoption services requested. There is often a concern of the perspective adoptive parents that the birth mother will change her mind at some point in the adoption process. This is possible however, after the birth of the child, the birth mother is required to legally sign over her custody of the child, after this is done her parental rights are terminated. The adoption process can be long and emotionally draining, however the reward of fulfilling the maternal and paternal desires can be well worth the effort.

Foster parenting is similar to adoption in that the foster parent acts as a surrogate parent for the child and it is a legitimate way to meet one's maternal or paternal desires. Foster parenting is different from adoption in that the foster parent is an agent of the state who cares for the child temporarily. Foster children are sometimes the result of birth parents giving them up for adoptions, the loss of custody due to incarceration, or a host of other reasons. Perspective foster parents go through a screening process that is similar to the adoption process. Once they are qualified they receive a stipend for every child they care for. Whether the choice is to adopt or to be a foster parent the decision should be made out of a sense of God's calling, not for selfish reasons. The decision should be agreed upon by both spouses because parenting is a team effort. Many states will allow single qualified adults to adopt and be foster parents. While the desire of a single adult to care for a child that is not their own is noble it is God's intention that the family have both a father and a mother. Single parenting is not God's preferred method of raising children, therefore singles adopting or having foster children should be discouraged. The single person who has a desire for children should ask God to open doors for them to work with children in their spiritual or secular vocation. They can also intimately care for the children of family and friends. If adoption or foster parenting is decided upon by a married couple it can be a rewarding experience for the parents as well as the children.

The Longing To Give Love and Comfort Unselfishly

The longing to give love and comfort unselfishly is part of our natural desire to sexually satisfy those we care about. In 2 Samuel 12:24 we are told that David comforted Bathsheba sexually after the loss of their first child and as a result of that union Solomon was conceived. David had been confronted by Nathan, the prophet, about his sin and he was told that he would not die but that adversity would be in his house as a result of his wrong doing. During Old Testament times both adultery and murder were capital offenses. Consider this: why didn't David suffer the ultimate consequence for his sin? The answer is found in the nature of God's grace and mercy. God spared David's life because He predetermined that Jesus would be in the lineage of David and He would not alter the plan He established in eternity. God did this to demonstrate that our strength is found in His purpose for our lives not our weaknesses. The penalty for David's sin was also mitigated because he was, "a man after God's own heart." This was demonstrated in his repentance once he was confronted with his sin. Although David was spared the full consequence of his sin the turmoil his family would suffer is proof that you can choose your sin, but you cannot choose the consequences of your sin.

Whether David was praising God or doing battle against the Philistines, he was a passionate man. It is natural for passionate people to express their love sexually just as David did. David and Bathsheba went through a critical time together, she lost her first husband and child, which no doubt created a bond of intimacy with David. It was natural for this emotional intimacy to express itself sexually. In the Song of Solomon 8:3 we are told:

> *His left hand is under my head, and his right*
> *hand embraces me. I charge you O daughters*
> *of Jerusalem do not stir up or awaken love*
> *until it pleases.*

Solomon was David's only child with Bathsheba. He wrote the Song of Solomon which is the most passionate book in the Bible. In the above passage of scripture, Solomon's lover describes one of her sexual encounters with him and she makes it clear that sex is nothing to play with. Sexual desires can be emotionally and physically overwhelming and they should only be awakened within the covenant of marriage. This is easier said than done, but it can be accomplished with much prayer and self-discipline.

I can identify with the sexual passion of David and Solomon. Both men expressed their love for women sexually. I can recall a time in my life where, to have a woman tell me thank you because she felt soft thunder in her head or that her body felt like the warm waves of the deepest ocean would make my day. But pure ego satisfaction can be just as shallow as pure physical satisfaction. Imagine this: what would sex be like with someone that you sensed the presence of God with and you loved them dearly? Add to that your physical attraction to them and you have a recipe for good sex. My point is that sex has so much more meaning when it is motivated by love with a desire to comfort your mate. We must recognize the gift God gave us, as humans, to enjoy sex as the ultimate expression of intimacy with our mates. Animals mate simply to procreate. Sex between a man and a woman often will not produce children, but it should always produce spiritual and emotional intimacy.

It is possible that you will not marry a person with the same sexual temperament as yourself and if this is the case your motive for sex should be pleasing your mate unselfishly. Inevitably, there will be times when one person desires sex and the other does not. This may be due to a physical or emotional infirmity that needs to be addressed with a medical professional. Sometimes the lack of sexual desire is as simple as physical fatigue from work or emotional fatigue from raising children, but when unconditional love is the true motive, there will be understanding that will bring the couple closer together. When we have sex out of a longing to give love and comfort unselfishly, we have an intimacy with our mates that should only be surpassed by our intimacy with God.

Summary

David and Bathsheba's relationship is an excellent example of how God can take our failures and turn them into success. David's lack of understanding his motivations for sex led to his adultery with Bathsheba. If David fully understood his longing to fulfill his physical, emotional, and paternal desire for sex he would have known that the most important motivation for sex is to give love and comfort unselfishly. Although David allowed his lust and pride to influence his sexual relationship with Bathsheba the end result was a man who had a repentant heart. David and Bathsheba's relationship started out in sin but it produced Solomon, who would grow to become the wisest king who ever lived. This does not justify sin because sin always has consequences but it gives us hope that in our sexual weaknesses God can ultimately get the honor and glory.

God intended for sex to be experienced between a man and a woman in the covenant of marriage. So often we hear, "Just say no" to sex if you are not married. Telling someone who enjoys sex to abstain is like telling someone who is overweight and enjoys food to go on a diet, it is not that simple. People struggle with their sexuality based on their sexual temperament. If you have a high sexual temperament abstinence will be difficult but if you have a low sexual temperament abstinence will be easy. There are people who have a high sexual temperament who have asked God to deliver them from their intense sexual desires and His response to them is, "My grace is sufficient for you." If you have fallen sexually get back up and try to walk again. God often allows intense sexual desires to teach us humility and remind us that any righteousness is not of ourselves but only in Him. Sexual abstinence can be maintained with prayer, self-discipline and walking with those who are going in the same direction.

Sex in marriage presents many challenges such as how frequently you should have sex with one another and whether or not to use contraception. If a couple cannot have children naturally there are other options available including adoption and foster care. The couple should make prayerful decisions together based on what they believe the will of God is for their relationship.

When either spouse neglects the sexual desires of the other they put their relationship at risk and expose their mate to the temptation to commit adultery. However, it is important to understand that sex used just to satisfy physical or emotional needs can be just as selfish as using sex simply to have children. Sex in marriage should have as its highest purpose expressing love and bringing comfort to your mate. When a man and a woman have vertical intimacy with God it will facilitate their horizontal intimacy with one another.

Conclusion

◆

Who is more important: the mail carrier or the person who sent the letter? Obviously there would be no letter without the sender. The sender simply used the mail carrier to accomplish his or her purpose. In the same way God desires to send us messages in the mail through the relationships He has ordained. He may send us a message of love through our family relationships. He may send a message of wisdom through our ministry relationships. He may send a message of integrity through our professional relationships, but regardless as to the message or type of relationship we need to value Him first and foremost.

We risk falling into error in our relationships not only when we do not keep God first but when we don't understand the purpose of the relationship. If I understand that my relationship with my mail carrier is primarily professional, I should not get upset if he or she does not make personal time to sit down and drink coffee with me. One of the best examples of a relationship was the friendship between Jonathan and David. Jonathan was heir to the throne of David, but understood God's own plan for David to be the next king. Therefore, Jonathan and David were able to have an extraordinary friendship because their relationship was like a strong building. God was their foundation and a common sense of purpose was the frame that caused their friendship to stand as an excellent example of a relationship.

Conversely, David's relationship with Bathsheba was at risk because he stepped outside of God's purpose for the relationship. David should have respected the fact that Bathsheba was not only another man's wife, but she was also one of his subjects as king. David's adultery with Bathsheba was not only immoral because she was married, but it was also unethical because he compromised his integrity as king. Likewise we should always consider the moral and ethical ramifications of our relationship choices.

It is my prayer that after reading *Risky Relationships* you will recognize and understand the risks you took in your past relationships while gaining wisdom for your current and future relationships. I believe that once we truly understand that all of our relationships are at risk apart from God and our purpose, we will be led to those relationships that will point us back to God with whom we should have our primary relationship.

The Most Important Relationship

When we behold the beauty of the sunrise, feel the cool breeze of a hot summer day, or listen to the melody of birds singing in the morning, we are witnessing the majesty of God and His creation. In all that God made He crowned man as the epitome of His creation because He desired relationship with those who would be made in His image and after His likeness. Although man was made in God's image he chose to disobey Him which opened the door for sin and death to enter the earth. God is a holy and righteous Creator who rewards obedience with life and punishes disobedience with death and separation from Him.

In the Old Testament God responded to man's disobedience with love and mercy by allowing him to atone for his sin through the sacrificial death of innocent animals. This system was imperfect because man had to offer sacrifices continually and they were only a shadow of the ultimate sacrifice God would offer on our behalf through His son, Jesus Christ. Jesus Christ was born not only to die for man's sin but to be a living example of how man can walk in grace and truth. The most important relationship we can have is with Jesus Christ through faith because He is the only way to God the Father.

When we open or hearts to Jesus Christ our perspective on life changes from a secular point of view to a spiritual point of view. If we are faithful to our vertical relationship with God it will be reflected in our horizontal relationship with others. In the final analysis all of our relationships will be better when we are committed to our most important relationship with Jesus Christ.

Selected Bibliography

Cunningham, Dane T. "Take a Look Within." Atlanta, GA. Embrace Relationships Seminars, Inc., 2002

Dimitrius, Jo-Ellan & Mazzarella, Mark. "Reading People." New York, N.Y. Ballantine Books, 1999

Getz, Gene. "David Seeking God Faithfully." Nashville, TN. Broadman & Holman Publishers, 1995

Long, Bishop Eddie L. "I Don't Want Delilah, I Need You." Tulsa, Ok. Albury Publishing, 1998

Piver, Susan. "The Hard Questions." New York, N.Y. Penguin Putnam Inc., 2000

Stewart, John & Logan, Carol. "Together Communicating Interpersonally." New York, N.Y. McGraw-Hill Inc., 1993

Talley, Jim & Reed, Bobbie. "Too Close Too Soon." Nashville, TN. Thomas Nelson Publishers, 1990

About the Author

꧁꧂

Dane T. Cunningham is the Founder and CEO of Embrace Relationships Seminars (ERS Inc.) ERS Inc. is a non-profit ministry that provides biblically based instruction through mediums such as seminars, books, videos, and tapes to assist individuals from all walks of life in enhancing, managing, and building relationships through accountability, communication, and encouragement. Dane is an ordained minister and serves in a dual capacity as an Elder and as the Singles Minister at New Birth Missionary Baptist Church in Lithonia, Georgia. He has previously served as a Christian Education Instructor and as the Director of the Ministers-In-Training program at New Birth. His secular career includes his current position of Sergeant with the Dekalb County Police Department in Decatur, Georgia, a State Trooper with the State of Ohio, and four years of military service with the United States Air Force where he was honorably discharged after attaining the rank of Sergeant.

He holds a certificate of Biblical Studies from Beulah Heights Bible College in Atlanta, Georgia. He is the author of *Take a Look Within* which is a biblical perspective on why we do what we do, and delights in serving the Lord by teaching God's Word and helping others to mature in Christ. Dane resides in Decatur, Georgia.

TO ORDER, RISKY RELATIONSHIPS

Phone: 1.866.381. BOOK (2665)
OR
Visit: www.xulonpress.com
OR
www.embrace-relationships.com

To request information
OR
For speaking engagements,
contact Dane T. Cunningham at:

EMBRACE RELATIONSHIPS SEMINARS INC.
P.O. BOX 370124
DECATUR, GA 30037

Phone: 770.908.3337
Fax: 404.759.2112

Printed in the United States
34186LVS00002B/54